CW00871376

Much Have I Travell'd

A Book of Quotations

Much Have I Travell'd

A Book of Quotations

Compiled by Kirsty Crawford

About Kirsty Crawford

Following her degree in English language and literature, Kirsty Crawford worked in book publishing for ten years before becoming a freelance editor and writer. She lives in London with her husband.

Cadogan Guides
Highlands House,
165 The Broadway,
London SW19 1NE
info.cadogan@virgin.net
www.cadoganguides.com

The Globe Pequot Press
246 Goose Lane,
PO Box 480, Guilford,
Connecticut 06437–0480

Editorial arrangement
© Cadogan Guides, 2003

Cover Photograph
© Jon Feingersh/CORBIS

Printed in Finland by WS Bookwell

A catalogue record for this book
is available from the British Library
ISBN 1-86011-133-5

All rights reserved. No part of this publication may be reproduced, stored in a retrieval system, or transmitted, in any form or by any means, electronic or mechanical, including photocopying and recording, or by any information storage and retrieval system except as may be expressly permitted in the UK 1988 Copyright Design & Patents Act and the USA 1976 Copyright Act or in writing from the publisher. Requests for permission should be addressed to Cadogan Guides, Highlands House, 165 The Broadway, London SW19 1NE, in the UK, or The Globe Pequot Press, 246 Goose Lane, PO Box 480, Guilford, Connecticut 06437–0480, in the USA.

Introduction

The title of this book is taken from Keats' poem 'On first looking into Chapman's Homer'. He likens his experience of reading to a voyage in realms of gold, and that seemed particularly apt for this collection of quotations. Travel has always been used not just to describe physical movement but also as metaphor for life and death. This book explores all meanings of travel, whether it is an actual voyage, an imaginative flight of fancy or a spiritual progress. There are epic adventures by explorers and seafarers, real and imagined, but also the musings of a poet or an Emperor. There are heroic feats, but also a child trailing up the stairs to bed, or an ordinary train ride.

Travel remained essentially the same for centuries: journeys were made on horseback, in a wagon, by a boat powered by oar or sail, or by foot. In only the last hundred or so years, methods of travel have transformed rapidly and almost beyond imagination. Now we drive cars, travel in the air and below the seas. We have broken the sound barrier and landed on the moon, climbed the highest mountains and reached the poles. We have changed our ability to travel and our attitude to it but, as the following quotations show, much has remained the same. The spirit of adventure is eternally renewing itself as new challenges present themselves: the ancient seafarers were charting the unknown in the same spirit of determination and courage as the space-travellers today. And, of course, travel is not all scaling peaks and conquering oceans. Lovers still part reluctantly and mourn the absence that travel enforces. Virgil remarks that singing makes a journey less tedious, while in Jane Austen's *Emma*, the much-anticipated outing to Box Hill falls short of the heroine's high expectations. We recognise these moments and they remain true across the ages that separate the travellers.

This collection could not hope to be definitive, and it does not pretend to be. It is not an anthology or a guide. Rather it is a journey across the ages, visiting the riches of travel that through time have reaped such intrepid and fascinating history, so much literature, poetry, wit and accumulated wisdom. The book seeks to be an enjoyable companion that celebrates travel in all its many forms and its great variety. It has been wonderful to compile – I hope it is as pleasurable to read.

Kirsty Crawford

Tell me, Muse, of the man of many resources, who wandered far and wide after he had sacked Troy's sacred city, and saw the towns of many men and learned their thoughts.

Homer (c.750-700BC)
The Odyssey, Book I

The dawn speeds a man on his journey, and speeds him too in his work

Hesiod (c.700BC)

Hesperus, you herd homeward whatever Dawn's light dispersed: you herd sheep – herd goats – herd children home to their mothers

Sappho (c. 612BC)
Fragment 120

Come, let us take our fill of love until the morning:
let us solace ourselves with loves.
For the goodman is not at home,
he is gone a long journey:

he hath taken a bag of money with him,
and will come home at the day appointed.

King James Bible
Proverbs 7

One may know the world without going out of doors

Lao Tzu (c.604-531BC)
The Way of Lao Tzu

Their ships are swift as a bird or a thought

Homer (c.750-700BC)
The Odyssey, Book VIII

Slow and steady wins the race

Aesop (c.620-560BC)
Fables

A journey of a thousand miles must begin with a single step of obedience to a call!

Lao Tzu (c.604-531BC)
The Way of Lao Tzu

The Ancients

A youth, when at home, should be filial, and abroad, respectful to his elders

Confucius (c.551-479BC)
The Confucian Analects, 1:6

A good traveller has no fixed plans and is not intent on arriving

Lao Tzu (c.604-531BC)
The Way of Lao Tzu

Grey-eyed Athena sent them a favourable breeze, a fresh west wind, singing over the wine-dark sea

Homer (c.750-700BC)
The Odyssey, Book II

With reason one can travel the world over; without it, it is hard to move an inch

Chinese proverb

I am not an Athenian or a Greek, but a citizen of the world

Socrates (469-399BC)
'Of Banishment', *Plutarch*

For lo! I see a herald from the shore
Draw hither, shadowed with the olive-wreath—
And thirsty dust, twin-brother of the clay,
Speaks plain of travel far and truthful news—

Aeschylus (c.525-456BC)
Agamemnon

Yea, though I walk through the valley of the shadow of death, I will fear no evil

King James Bible
Psalm 23

I was left to wander through the world with a stricken heart, till the gods put an end to my sufferings and the day came, in the rich land of the Phaecians, when you comforted me with your talk and yourself guided me to their city.

But now I beseech you in your Father's name – since I cannot believe that I have come to my bright Ithaca but feel that I must be wandering in some foreign country and that you spoke to me as you did in a spirit of provocation to lead me astray – tell me, am I really back in my own beloved land?

Homer (c.750-700BC)
The Odyssey, Book XIII

The man of wisdom delights in water; the man of humanity delights in mountains. The man of wisdom is active; the man of humanity is tranquil.

Confucius (c.551-479BC)
The Confucian Analects 6:21

Then we turned, and took our journey into the wilderness by the way of the Red Sea, as the Lord spake unto me: and we compassed Mount Se'ir many days. And the Lord spake unto me, saying, Ye have compassed this mountain long enough: turn you northward.

King James Bible
Deutoronomy 2: 1-3

The road up and the road down are one and the same

Heraclitus (c. 540-480BC)

Favourite of Zeus, son of Laertes, Odysseus, master of strategum, what next, dauntless man? What greater exploit can you plan to surpass your voyage here? How did you dare to come below to Hades' realm, where the dead live on as mindless disembodied ghosts?

Homer (c.750-700BC)
The Odyssey, Book II

On a journey of a hundred miles, ninety is but half way

Chinese proverb

Walking is man's best medicine

Hippocrates (c.460-370BC)

These are the journeys of the children of Israel, which went forth out of the land of Egypt with their armies under the hand of Moses and Aaron. And Moses wrote their goings out according to their journeys by the commandment of the Lord: and these are their journeys according to their goings out. And they departed from Ram'eses in the first month, on the fifteenth day of the first month; on the morrow after the passover the children of Israel went out with a high hand in the sight of all the Egyptians.

King James Bible
Numbers 33: 1-3

The descent to Hades is the same from every place

Anaxagoras (c.500-428BC)
Diogenes Laertius, *Anaxagoras*, VI

What greater grief than the loss of one's native land

Euripides (484-406BC)
Medea, L.650

And your children shall wander in the wilderness forty years

King James Bible
Numbers 14: 33

Stranger in a strange country

Sophocles (c.496-406BC)
Oedipus at Colonus

With their generals arrested and the captain and soldiers who had gone with them put to death, the Greeks were in an extremely awkward position...They were at least a thousand miles away from Greece; they had no guide to show them the way; they were shut in by impassable rivers which traversed their homeward journey; even the natives who had marched on the capital with Cyrus had turned against them, and they were left by themselves without a single cavalryman in their army, so that it was evident that, if they won a victory, they could not kill any of their enemies, and if they were defeated themselves, none of them would be left alive.

Xenephon (c.4th century BC)
The Persian Expedition

And the Lord went before them by day in a pillar of a cloud, to lead them the way; and by night in a pillar of fire, to give them light; to go by day and night. He took not away the pillar of the cloud by day, nor the pillar of fire by night, from before the people.

King James Bible
Exodus 13:21,22

In soft regions are born soft men

Herodotus (c.484-432BC)
Histories, Book IX

I would win my way to the coast,
Apple-bearing Hesperian coast
Of which minstrels sing,
Where the Lord of the Ocean
Denies the voyage further sailing,
And fixes the solemn limit of Heaven
Which the giant Atlas upholds.

Euripides (c.484-406BC)
Hippolytus L.787-793

Now, when they are coming to the city of Bubastis they do as follows:—they sail men and women together, and a great multitude of each sex in every boat; and some of the women have rattles and rattle with them, while some of the men play the flute during the whole time of the voyage, and the rest, both women and men, sing and clap their hands; and when as they sail they come opposite to any city on the way they bring the boat to land, and some of the women continue to do as I have said, others cry aloud and jeer at the women in that city, some dance, and some stand up and pull up their garments. This they do by every city along the river-bank; and when they come to Bubastis they hold a festival celebrating great sacrifices, and more wine of grapes is consumed upon that festival than during the whole of the rest of the year.

Herodotus (c.484-432BC)
Histories, BOOK II, on Egypt

The road to Hades is easy to travel

Bion (c.325-255BC)
Diogenes Laertius, *Bion*, III

An exile's life is no life

Leonides of Tarentum (c.290-220BC)

The longest part of the journey is said to be the passing of the gate

Marcus Terentius Varro (116-27BC)
On Agriculture, Book I

What is more agreeable than one's home?

Marcus Tullius Cicero (106-43BC)
Ad Familiares, Book IV

Let us go singing as far as we go: the road will be less tedious

Virgil (70-19BC)
Eclogues, IX

In Rome you long for the country: in the country – oh inconstant! – you praise the distant city to the stars.

Horace (65-8BC)
Satires, II

Much Have I Travell'd

May the countryside and the gliding valley streams content me. Lost to fame, let me love river and woodland.

Virgil (70-19BC)
Georgics, II

Tomorrow, once again, we sail the Ocean Sea

Horace (65-8BC)
Odes, I

A great pilot can sail even when his canvas is rent

Seneca (5BC-65AD)
Epistles, XXX

It is not everyone that can get to Corinth

Horace (65-8BC)
Epistles, I

If a man does not know to what port he is steering, no wind is favourable to him.

Seneca (c.5BC-65AD)
Epistulae ad Lucilium, 73

They change their clime, not their disposition, who run across the sea

Horace (65-8BC)
Epistles, I

There is always something new out of Africa

Pliny the Elder (23-79AD)
Natural History, VIII

We most often go astray on a well trodden and much frequented road.

Seneca (5BC-65AD)

Now I will come unto you, when I shall pass through Macedonia: for I do pass through Macedonia. And it may be that I will abide, yea, and winter with you, that ye may bring me on my journey whithersoever I go. For I will not see you now by the way; but I trust to tarry a while with you, if the Lord permit. But I will tarry at Ephesus until Pentecost.

King James Bible
Corinthians 15:5-8

His departure was effected by Nicogenes by the following artifice; the barbarous nations, and amongst them the Persians especially, are extremely jealous, severe, and suspicious about their women, not only their wives, but also their bought slaves and concubines, whom they keep so strictly that no one ever sees them abroad; they spend their lives shut up within doors, and, when they take a journey, are carried in close tents, curtained in on all sides, and set upon a wagon. Such a travelling carriage being prepared for Themistocles, they hid him in it, and carried him on his journey, and told those whom they met or spoke with upon the road that they were conveying a young Greek woman out of Ionia to a nobleman at court.

Plutarch (c.46–120AD)
'Themistocles', *Plutarch's Lives*

I came, I saw, I conquered.
Julius Caesar (100-44BC)

Travel light and you can sing in the robber's face

Juvenal (55-127AD)
Satires, X

And he said unto them, Take nothing for your journey, neither staves, nor scrip, neither bread, neither money; neither have two coats apiece. And whatsoever house ye enter into, there abide, and thence depart. And whosoever will not receive you, when ye go out of that city, shake off the very dust from your feet for a testimony against them.

King James Bible
Luke 9: 3-5

Aided by a favourable wind, we voyaged many days and nights and at length came to Basrah and thence to Baghdad, the City of Peace. I conveyed to my stores the valuables I had brought with me, and taking my wife to my own house in my old street, rejoiced to meet my kinsfolk and my old companions. They told me that this voyage had kept me abroad for nearly twenty-seven years, and marvelled exceedingly at all that had befallen me.

I rendered deep thanks to Allah for bringing me safely back to my friends and kinsfolk and solemnly vowed never to travel again by sea or land.

Anonymous
'The Seven Voyages of Sinbad the Sailor' from
Tales from the Thousand and One Nights

An agreeable companion on a journey is as good as a carriage.

Publius Syrus (42BC)
Maxim, 143

Meantime the Trojan cuts his wat'ry way,
Fix'd on his voyage, thro' the curling sea

Virgil (70–19BC)
Æneid, Book V

As on the high road he who walks lightest walks with most ease, so on the journey of life more happiness comes from lightening the needs by poverty than from panting under a burden of wealth.

Marcus Minucius Felix (c.2nd century AD)
Octavius, 36

If the wind will not serve, take to the oars.

Latin proverb

The Germans, I am apt to believe, derive their origin from no other people; and are in no way mixed with different nations arriving amongst them: since anciently those who went in search of new buildings, travelled not by land, but were carried in fleets; and into that mighty ocean so boundless, and, as I may call it, so repugnant and forbidding, ships from our world rarely enter. Moreover, besides the dangers from a sea tempestuous, horrid and unknown, who would relinquish Asia, or Africa, or Italy, to repair to Germany, a region hideous and rude, under a rigorous climate, dismal to behold or to manure unless the same were his native country?

Tacitus (c.55-117AD)
On Germany

Off you go, madman, and hurry across the horrible Alps, duly to delight schoolboys and become a subject for practising speech-making.

Juvenal (55-127AD)
On Hannibal, Satires, x

Anyone can hold the helm when the sea is calm.

Publius Syrus (c.42BC)
Maxim, 358

Now he goes along the darksome road, from where they say no one returns

Catullus (c.84–54BC)
Carmina, 4

To know the road ahead, ask those coming back

Chinese proverb

Men seek for seclusion in the wilderness, by the seashore, or in the mountains – a dream you have cherished only too fondly yourself. But such fancies are wholly unworthy of a philosopher, since at any moment you choose you can retire within yourself.

Marcus Aurelius (d.180)
Meditations, IV

'What sudden panic is this,' he said, 'which has entered those breasts where fear has never been? Year after year you have fought with me, and won; and you never left Spain until all the lands and peoples between the two seas were subject to our power. When the Roman people demanded the surrender of the "criminal" – whoever it might have been – who laid siege to Saguntum, you were justly angry and crossed the Ebro bent upon obliterating the very name of Rome and setting the world free. Then, at least, none of you thought the journey long, though it stretched from the setting to the rising sun; but now you can see that much the greater part of the distance is already behind you – when you made your way over the passes of the Pyrenees, when you have tamed the violence of the mighty Rhône and crossed it in the face of countless Gallic warriors who would have stopped you; when, finally, you have the Alps in sight, and know that the other side of them is Italian soil: now, I repeat, at the very gateway to the enemy's country, you come to a halt – exhausted! What do you think the Alps are? Are they anything worse than high mountains? Say, if you will, that they are higher than the Pyrenees, but what of it? No part of earth reaches the sky; no height is unsuperable to men. Moreover, the Alps are not desert: men live there, they till the ground; there are animals there, living creatures. If a small party can cross them, surely armies can?... Surely, then, for an army of soldiers, with nothing to carry but their military gear, no waste should be too wild to cross, no hills too high to climb.'

Livy (59BC-17AD)
Hannibal's Crossing of the Alps

Press steadily on, keep to the straight road in your thinking and doing, and your days will ever flow on smoothly.

Marcus Aurelius (d.180)
Meditations

They that go down to the sea in ships,
that do business in great waters;
these see the works of the Lord,
and his wonders in the deep.
For he commandeth, and raiseth the stormy
wind,
which lifteth up the waves thereof.
They mount up to the heaven,
they go down again to the depths:
their soul is melted because of trouble.
They reel to and fro,
and stagger like a drunken man,
and are at their wit's end.
Then they cry unto the Lord in their trouble,
and he bringeth them out of their distresses.
He maketh the storm a calm,
so that the waves thereof are still.
Then are they glad because they be quiet:
so he bringeth them unto their desired haven.

Oh that men would praise the Lord for his goodness,
and for his wonderful works to the children of men!

King James Bible
Psalm 107

King Pelias stood up in the hall and holding up his sceptre he said, 'O my nephew Jason, and O friends assembled here, I promise that I will have built for the voyage the best ship that ever sailed from a harbour in Greece. And I promise that I will send throughout all Greece a word telling of Jason's voyage so that all heroes desirous of winning fame may come to help him and to help all of you who may go with him to win from the keeping of King Æetes the famous Fleece of Gold.'

So King Pelias said, but Jason, looking to the king from his father's stricken eyes, saw that he had been led by the king into the acceptance of the voyage so that he might fare far from Iolcus, and perhaps lose his life in striving to gain the wonder that King Æetes kept guarded. By the glitter in Pelias's eyes he knew the truth. Nevertheless Jason would not take back one word that he had spoken; his heart was strong within him, and he thought that with the help of the bright-eyed youths around and with the help of those who would come to him at the word of the voyage, he would bring the Golden Fleece to Iolcus and make famous for all time his own name.

Padraic Colum (1881-1972)
The Golden Fleece and the Heroes Who Lived before Achilles. Part 1, ch. 3

To lie about a far country is easy

Amharic proverb

A little while, and all that is before your eyes now will have perished. Those who witness its passing will go the same road themselves before too long; and then what will there be to choose between the oldest grandfather and the baby that died in its cradle?

Marcus Aurelius (d.180)
Meditations

For it is not by our feet, or change of place, that men leave Thee, or return unto Thee. Or did that

Thy younger son look out for horses or chariots, or ships, fly with visible wings, or journey by the motion of his limbs, that he might in a far country waste in riotous living all Thou gavest at his departure? a loving Father, when Thou gavest, and more loving unto him, when he returned empty. So then in lustful, that is, in darkened affections, is the true distance from Thy face.

St Augustine (354-430)
Confessions

O, happy was that long lost age
Content with nature's faithful fruits...
Men did not plunder all the world
And cut a path across the seas
With merchandise for foreign shores.

Boethius (c.475-525)
The Consolation of Philosophy, Book II

Keep on adding, keep on walking, keep on progressing: do not delay on the road, do not go back, do not deviate.

St Augustine (354-430)

Hard is the journey,
Hard is the journey,
So many turnings,
And now where am I?

Li Po (701-762)
'Hard is the Journey'

Men go out to admire the heights of mountains, the huge waves of the sea, the broadest spans of rivers, the circle of ocean, the revolutions of stars, and leave themselves behind.

St Augustine (354-430)

Let the brethren who are sent on a journey commend themselves to the prayers of all the brethren and of the Abbot;
and always at the last prayer of the Work of God let a commemoration be made of all absent brethren.

St Benedict (c.628-690)
Rule of St Benedict, ch.67

It is Spring in the mountains.
I come alone seeking you

Tu Fu (712-770)
'Written On The Wall At Chang's Hermitage'

White King City I left at dawn
in the morning-glow of the clouds;
The thousand miles to Chiang-ling
we sailed in a single day.
On either shore the gibbons' chatter
sounded without pause
While my light boat skimmed past
ten thousand sombre crags.

Li Po (701-762)
'Leaving White King City'

Here halt, I pray you, make a little stay
O wayfarer, to read what I have writ
And know by my fate what thy fate shall be.
What thou art now, wayfarer, world renowned,
I was: what I am now, so shall thou be.
The world's delight I followed with a heart
Unsatisfied: ashes am I, and dust.

Alcuin (c.735-804)
'Epitaph'

When brethren return from a journey,
at the end of each canonical Hour of the Work of God
on the day they return,
let them lie prostrate on the floor of the oratory
and beg the prayers of all
on account of any faults
that may have surprised them on the road,
through the seeing or hearing of something evil,
or through idle talk.
And let no one presume to tell another
whatever he may have seen or heard outside of the monastery,
because this causes very great harm.

St Benedict (c.628-690)
Rule of St Benedict, ch.67

Even now my heart
Journeys beyond its confines, and my thoughts
Over the sea, across the whale's domain,
Travel afar the regions of the earth,
And then come back to me with greed and longing.

Anonymous Anglo-Saxon poem
(c. 8th century)
'The Seafarer'

The Island Britain was unknown to the Romans until Caius Cesar, by surname Julius, sought it with an army, and subdued it, sixty winters ere Christ's coming.

King Alfred the Great (849-899)
Bede's Ecclesiastical History, ch. 2

The Angles and the Saxons came from the east,
Over the broad sea sought the land of Britain,
Conquered the Welsh and so obtained this land.

Anonymous Anglo-Saxon poem
(c. 8th century)
'The Battle of Brunaburh'

Before the journey that awaits us all,
No man becomes so wise that he has not
Need to think out, before his going hence,
What judgement will be given to his soul
After his death, of evil or of good.

Anonymous Anglo-Saxon poem (c. 735)
'Bede's Death Song'

Britain is an island of the ocean which of yore named Albion and is set betwixt North-deal and West-deal, at a great distance over against Germany, Gaul and Spain, the largest divisions of Europe; that is North eight hundred miles long, and West two hundred miles broad.

King Alfred the Great (849-899)
Bede's Ecclesiastical History, ch. 1

In that time, in all this land,
Not one acre of land there was found,
No town, nor house, never one
When Brutus then from Troy was come.
All was wood and wilderness
Here nothing was tilled, more or less.
Giants lived here, exceeding strong,
That were both great and long
Gogmagog was their king
He never had an equal.
He was of such great strength
Forty foot he was in length.

Anonymous (c. 8th century)
Short English Chronicle

Then Beowulf strode,
glad of his gold-gifts, the grass-plot o'er,
warrior blithe. The wave-roamer bode
riding at anchor, its owner awaiting.
As they hastened onward, Hrothgar's gift
they lauded at length.—'Twas a lord unpeered,
every way blameless, till age had broken
—it spareth no mortal—his splendid might.
Came now to ocean the ever-courageous
hardy henchmen, their harness bearing,
woven war-sarks. The warden marked,
trusty as ever, the earl's return.
From the height of the hill no hostile words
reached the guests as he rode to greet them;
but 'Welcome!' he called to that Weder clan
as the sheen-mailed spoilers to ship marched on.
Then on the strand, with steeds and treasure
and armour their roomy and ring-dight ship
was heavily laden: high its mast
rose over Hrothgar's hoarded gems.
A sword to the boat-guard Beowulf gave,
mounted with gold; on the mead-bench since
he was better esteemed, that blade possessing,
heirloom old.—Their ocean-keel boarding,
they drove through the deep, and Daneland left.

Anonymous Anglo-Saxon poem
(c. 8th century)
Beowulf

Since long ago I wrapped my lord's remains
In the darkness of the earth, and sadly thence
Journeyed by winter over icy waves,
And suffering sought the hall of a new patron
If I in any land might find one willing
To show me recognition in his mead-hall.
Comfort my loneliness, tempt me with pleasures.

Anonymous Anglo-Saxon poem
(c. 8th century)
'The Wanderer'

You will find something more in woods than in books. Trees and stones will teach you that which you can never learn from masters.

St Bernard of Clairvaux (1090-1153)
Epistles 6

In the middle of the journey of our life, I woke to find myself within a dark wood where the way was straight.

Dante Aligheri (1265–1321)
'Inferno', I, *The Divine Comedy*

The world nys but a thurghfare ful of wo
And we been pilgrymess, passing to and fro.

Geoffrey Chaucer (c.1343-1400)
'The Knight's Tale', *The Canterbury Tales*

It is now the hour that turns back the longing of seafarers and melts their hearts, the day they have bidden dear friends farewell, and pierces the new traveller with love if he hears in the distance the bell that seems to mourn the dying day.

Dante Aligheri (1265-1321)
'Purgatorio', VIII, *The Divine Comedy*

I wol nat longe holde you in fable
Of al this garden dilectable.
I mot my tonge stynten nede,
For I ne may, withouten drede,
Naught tellen you the beaute al,
Ne half the bounte therewithal.
I went on right hond and on left
About the place; it was nat left
Tyl I had [in] al the garden ben,
In the estres that men myghte sen.

Geoffrey Chaucer (c.1343-1400)
Romaunt of the Rose

I believe it was God's will that we should come back, so that men might know the things that are in the world, since, as we have said in the first chapter of this book, no other man, Christian or Saracen, Mongol or pagan, has explored so much of the world as Master Marco, son of Master Niccolo Polo, great and noble citizen of the city of Venice.

Marco Polo (1254-1324)
The Travels

I, John Mandeville, Knight, albeit I be not unworthy, that was born in England, in the town of St Albans and passed the sea in the year of our Lord Jesu Christ, 1332, On St Michelmas Day; and hitherto have been long time over the sea, and have seen and gone through many diverse lands, and many provinces and kingdoms and isles and have passed throughout Turkey, Armenia the little and the great; through Tartary, Persia, Syria, Arabia, Egypt the high and the low; through Lybia, Chaldea, and a great part of Ethiopia; through Amazonia, Ind the less and the more, a great part; and throughout many other isles that be about Ind; where dwell many diverse folks, and of diverse manners and laws, and of diverse shapes of men.

Sir John Mandeville (c.1300-1372)
Prologue, *The Travels of Sir John Mandeville*

Of al this world the large compas
Yt wil not in myn armes tweyne;
Who so mochel wol embrace,
Litel thereof he shal distreyne

Geoffrey Chaucer (c.1343-1400)
Proverbe of Chaucer

In a summer season, when soft was the sun,
I dressed myself in garments as though I were a sheep,
In clothes like those of an unholy hermit,
And travelled wide in this world to hear of wonders.

William Langland (c.1330-1387)
Prologue, *The Vision of Piers Plowman*

Now the gallant Sir Gawain in God's name goes
Riding through the realm of Britain, no rapture in his mind.
Often the long night he lay alone and companionless
And did not find in front of him the food of his choice;

He had no comrade but his courser in the country woods and hills,
No traveller to talk to on the track but God,
Until he was nearly nigh to Northern Wales.

Anonymous Anglo-Saxon poem
(c. 14th century)
'Sir Gawain and the Green Knight'

For many men have great liking, to hear speak of strange things of diverse countries

Sir John Mandeville (c.1300-1372)
The Travels of Sir John Mandeville

For a small reward a man will hurry away on a long journey, while for eternal life many will hardly take a single step.

Thomas à Kempis (1380-1471)

The longitude of a climat is a lyne ymagined fro est to west ilike distant fro the equinoxiall. And the latitude of a climat may be cleped the space of the erthe from the begynnyng of the first clymat unto the verrey ende of the same clymat evene direct ageyns the pool artyke. Thus sayn somme auctours; and somme of hem sayn that yf men clepe the latitude of a cuntrey the arch meridian that is contened or intercept bitwix the ceynth and the equinoxal, than say they that the distance fro the equinxial unto the ends of a clymat evene ageynst the pool artik is the latitude of a clymat forsooth.

Geoffrey Chaucer (c.1343-1400)
A Treatise on the Astrolabe, 39

When a man is riding through this desert by night and for some reason - falling asleep or anything else - he gets separated from his companions and wants to rejoin them, he hears spirit voices talking to him as if they were his companions, sometimes even calling him by name. Often these voices lure him away from the path and he never finds it again, and many travellers have got lost and died because of this. Sometimes in the night travellers hear a noise like the clatter of a great company of riders away from the road; if they believe that these are some of their own company and head for the noise, they find themselves in deep trouble when daylight comes and they realize their mistake.

There were some who, in crossing the desert, have seen a host of men coming towards them and, suspecting that they were robbers, returning, they have gone hopelessly astray... Even by daylight men hear these spirit voices, and often you fancy you are listening to the strains of many instruments, especially drums, and the clash of arms. For this reason bands of travellers make a point of keeping very close together. Before they go to sleep they set up a sign pointing in the direction in which they have to travel, and round the necks of all their beasts they fasten little bells, so that by listening to the sound they may prevent them from straying off the path.

Marco Polo (1254-1324)
The Travels

Whan that April with his showres soote
The droughte of March hath perced to the roote,
And bathed every veine in swich licour,
Of which vertu engendered is the flowr;
Whan Zephyrus eek with his sweete breeth
Inspired hath in every holt and heeth
The tendre croppes, and the yonge sonne
Hath in the Ram his halve cours yronne,
And smale fowles maken melodye
That sleepen al the night with open ye—

So priketh hem Nature in hir courages—
Thanne longen folk to goon on pilgrimages,
And palmeres for to seeken straunge strondes
To fern halwes, couthe in sondry londes;

Geoffrey Chaucer (c.1343-1400)
Prologue, *Canterbury Tales*

Who that is besy to mesure and compace
The hevyn and erth and all the worlde large
Descrybynge the clymatis and folke of every
place
He is a fole and hath a grevous charge,
Without avauntage...

Alexander Barclay (c.1475-1552)
The Ship of Folys

And Y adoun gan loken thoo,
And beheld feldes and playnes,
And now hills, and now mountaynes,
Now valeyes, now forests,
And now unnethes grete bestes,
Now ryveres, now citees,
Now tounes, and now grete trees,
Now shippes seyllynge in the see.
But thus sone in a while he

Was flown fro the ground so hye
That al the world, as to myn ye,
No more semed than a prikke;
Or elles was the air so thikke
That y ne myghte not discerne.

Geoffrey Chaucer (c.1343-1400)
The House of Fame L. 896-909 - an eagle takes the narrator on an amazing flight

The whole Countrey differeth very much from it selfe, by reason of the yeere: so that a man would marvaile to see the great alteration and difference betwixt the Winter and the Summer in Russia. The whole Countrey in the Winter lyeth under Snow, which falleth continually, and is sometimes of a yard or two thicke but greater towards the North...Divers not onely that travell abroad, but are in the very Market, and streets of their Townes, are mortally pinched and killed withall: so that you shall see many drop downe in the Streets, many Travellers brought into the Townes sitting dead and stiffe in their Sleds. Divers lose their Noses, the tippes of their Eares, and the balls of their Cheekes, their Toes, Feets, etc.

Dr Giles Fletcher (c.1589)
'A Treatise of Russia' in *Purchas His Pilgrims*

Thus the king with his great army departed, leaving the queen and realm in the governance of Sir Baudwin and Constantine. And when he was on his horse he said with an high voice, 'If I die in this journey I will that Sir Constantine be mine heir and king crowned of this realm as next of my blood', and after departed and entered into the sea at Sandwich with all his army, with a great multitude of ships, galleys, cogs, and dromonds, sailing on the sea.

Sir Thomas Malory (c.1405-1471)
Le Morte d'Arthur, Book 5, ch. 3

There are other lands – if anyone wished to travel through them – by which men could travel right round the earth, and return, if they had the grace of God to keep to the right route, to their native countries which they set out from. So, in time, they would girdle the earth. But it would be a very long time before such a voyage was finished; and few men try it, because there are so many dangers, by sea and by land, besetting men who travel in foreign lands which would most likely fall on those who intended to make that long journey of circumnavigation.

Sir John Mandeville
The Travels of Sir John Mandeville (c. 1300-1372)

There is no land unhabitable nor sea unnavigable

Robert Thorne (d. 1527)
Richard Hakluyt, *The Principal Navigations, Voyages and Discoveries of the English Nation*

London, thou art the flower of cities all.

William Dunbar (c.1465-1520)
London

While the better sort of us were seriously occupied in repairing our wants, and contriving of matters for the commodity of our voyage, others of another sort and disposition were plotting of mischief; some casting to steal away our shipping by night, watching opportunity by the General's and captains' lying on the shore; whose conspiracies discovered, they were prevented. Others drew together in company, and carried away out of the harbours adjoining a ship laden with fish, setting the poor men on shore. A great many more of our people stole into the woods to hide themselves, attending time and means to return home by such shipping as daily departed from the coast. Some were sick of fluxes, and many dead; and in brief, by one means or other our company was diminished, and many by the General licensed to return home. Insomuch as after we had reviewed our people, resolved to see an end of our voyage, we grew scant of men to furnish all our shipping; it seemed good therefore unto the General to leave the *Swallow* with such provision as might be spared for transporting home the sick people.

Edward Haies (c.1583)
Sir Humphrey Gilbert's Voyage to Newfoundland

If thy heart fails thee, climb not at all

Elizabeth I (1533-1603)
Thomas Fuller, *Worthies of England*

Travel, in the younger sort, is a part of education; in the elder, a part of experience. He that travelleth into a country before he hath some entrance into the language, goes to school, and not to travel.

Sir Francis Bacon (1561-1626)
'Of Travel', *Essays*

At two hours after midnight appeared the land, at a distance of two leagues. They hauled down the sails and set the treo, which is the main sail without bonnets, and lay to waiting for daylight Friday when they arrived at an island of the Bahamas that was called in the Indians' tongue Guanahani [San Salvador]. The Admiral called to the two captains and to the others who had jumped ashore and to Rodrigo Descobedo, the escrivano of the whole fleet, and to Rodrigo Sanchez de Segovia; and he said that they should be witnesses that, in the presence of all, he would take, as in fact he did take, possession of the said island for the king and for the queen, his lords, making the declarations that were required, and which at more length are contained in the testimonials made there in writing.

Christopher Columbus (1451-1506)
Journal of the First Voyage

You gentlemen of England
Who live at home in ease,
Ah! Little do you think upon
The danger of the seas.

Martin Parker (c.1600-1656)
'The Valiant Sailors'

Over hill, over dale,
Thorough bush, thorough brier,
Over park, over pale,
Thorough flood, thorough fire,
I do wander every where.
Swifter than the moon's sphere;
And I serve the Fairy Queen,
To dew her orbs upon the green.

William Shakespeare (1564-1616)
A Midsummer Night's Dream, Act 2, scene 1

Direct your eyesight inward, and you'll find
A thousand regions in your mind
Yet undiscover'd. Travel them, and be
Expert in home cosmography.

William Habington (1605-1654)
'To My Honoured Friend Sir Ed. P. Knight'
Castara

I have a long journey to take, and must bid the company farewell

Sir Walter Ralegh (c.1552-1618)
Last words

Why didst thou promise such a beauteous day
And make me travel forth without my cloak,
To let base clouds o'ertake me in my way,
Hiding thy bravery in their rotten smoke?

William Shakespeare (1564-1616)
Sonnet 34

England is the paradise of women, the purgatory of men, and the hell of horses.

John Florio (c.1553-1625)
Second Futes, ch.12

Know most of the rooms of thy native country
Before thou goest over the threshold thereof.

Thomas Fuller (1608-1661)
'Of Travelling', *The Holy State and the Profane State*

See one promontory (said Socrates of old), one mountain, one sea, one river, and see all.

Robert Burton (1577-1640)
The Anatomy of Melancholy

Who would fardel bear,
To grunt and sweat under a weary life,
But that the dread of something after death,
The undiscovered country from whose bourn
No traveller returns, puzzles the will,
And makes us rather bear those ills we have,
Than fly to others we know not of?

William Shakespeare (1564-1616)
Hamlet, Act 3, scene 1

It was no summer progress. A cold coming, they had of it, at this time of the year; just the worst time of the year, to take a journey, and specially a long journey, in. The ways deep, the weather sharp, the days short, the sun fartherest off *in solistio brumali*, the very dead of Winter.

Launcelot Andrewes (1555-1626)
'Of the Nativity', *Sermon*

The west yet glimmers with some streaks of day:
Now spurs the weary traveller apace
To gain the homely inn.

William Shakespeare (1564-1616)
Macbeth, Act 3, scene 4

There is in the universe neither centre nor circumference

Giordano Bruno (1548-1600)
On the Infinite Universe and Worlds

Sweet Valentine, adieu!
Think on thy Proteus, when thou haply seest
Some rare note-worthy object in thy travel:
Wish me partaker in thy happiness
When thou dost meet good hap; and in thy danger,
If ever danger do environ thee,
Commend thy grievance to my holy prayers,
For I will be thy beadsman, Valentine.

William Shakespeare (1564-1616)
Two Gentlemen of Verona, Act 1, scene 1

He disdains all things above his reach, and preferreth all countries before his own.

Sir Thomas Overbury (1581-1613)
'An Affected Traveller', *Miscellaneous Works*

How many weary steps,
Of many weary miles you have o'ergone,
Are number'd in the travel of one mile?

William Shakespeare (1564-1616)
Love's Labours Lost, Act 5, scene 2

It is a strange thing, that in sea voyages, where there is nothing to be seen but sky and sea, men should make diaries; but in land-travel, wherein so much is to be observed, for the most part they omit it; as if chance were fitter to be registered than observation.

Sir Francis Bacon (1561-1626)
'Of Travel', *Essays*

Dazel'd thus, with height of place,
Whilst our hopes our wits beguile,
No man markes the narrow space
'Twixt a prison and a smile.

Sir Henry Wotton (1568-1639)
'Upon the Sudden Restraint of the Earle of Somerset, then Falling from Favour'

When I was at home, I was in a better place; but travellers must be content.

William Shakespeare (1564-1616)
As You Like It, Act 2, scene 4

Dar'st thou aid mutinous Dutch, and dar'st thou lay
Thee in ships woodden Sepulchers, a prey
To leaders rage, to stormes, to shot, to dearth?
Dar'st thou dive seas, and dungeons of the earth?
Hast thou couragious fire to thaw the ice
Of frozen North discoveries?

John Donne (1572-1631)
'Satyre: Of Religion'

We are as near to Heaven by sea or by land.

Sir Humphrey Gilbert (c.1539-1583)
Richard Hakluyt, *Third and Last Volume of the Voyages...of the English Nation*

Praise the sea; on shore remain.

John Florio (c.1553-1625)
Second Frutes

Happy he who like Ulysses has made a glorious voyage

Joachim du Bellay (c.1522-1560)
Les Regrets

Our bodily eye findeth never an end, but is vanquished by the immensity of space.

Giordano Bruno (1548-1600)
On the Infinite Universe and Worlds

Secret thoughts and open countenance will go safely over the whole world.

Scipione Alberti
Cited in a letter from Sir Henry Wotton to John Milton, 13 April 1638

Full fathom five thy father lies;
Of his bones are coral made;
Those are pearls that were his eyes;
Nothing of him that doth fade
But doth suffer a sea-change
Into something rich and strange.

William Shakespeare (1564-1616)
The Tempest, Act 1, scene 2

Journey all over the universe in a map, without the expense and fatigue of travelling, without suffering the inconveniences of heat, cold, hunger and thirst.

Cervantes (1547-1616)
Don Quixote

It is a melancholy of mine own, compounded of many simples, extracted from many objects, and indeed the sundry contemplation of my travels, which by often rumination, wraps me in a most humorous sadness.

William Shakespeare (1564-1616)
Comedy of Errors, Act 1, scene 4

Give me my scallop shell of quiet
My staff of faith to walk upon
My scrip of joy, immortal diet,
My bottle of salvation
My gown of glory, hope's true gage,
And thus I'll make my pilgrimage.

Sir Walter Ralegh (c.1552-1618)
'The Passionate Man's Pilgrimage', *Diaphantus*

A gentle knight was pricking on the plain

Edmund Spenser (1552-1599)
The Faerie Queen, Book 1

Be valiant but not too venturous

John Lyly (c.1554-1606)
The Antatomy of Wit

The fifth of June, being in 43 degrees towards the pole Arctic, we found the air so cold, that our men being grievously pinched with the same, complained of the extremity thereof; and the further we went, the more the cold increased upon us. Whereupon we thought it best for that time to seek the land, and did so; finding it not mountainous, but low plain land, till we came within 38 degrees towards the line. In which height it pleased God to send us into a fair and good bay, with a good wind to enter the same. In this bay we anchored; and the people of the country, having their houses close by the water's side, shewed themselves unto us, and sent a present to our General. When they came unto us, they greatly wondered at the things that we brought. But our General, according to his natural and accustomed humanity, courteously intreated them, and liberally bestowed on them necessary things to cover their nakedness; whereupon they supposed us to be gods, and would not be persuaded to the contrary.

Francis Pretty (c.1581)
Sir Francis Drake's Famous Voyage Round the World

Fair stood the wind for France

Michael Drayton (1563-1631)
'The Ballad of Agincourt'

They are never alone that are accompanied with noble thoughts

Sir Philip Sidney (1554-1586)
Arcadia, BOOK 1

They are ill discoverers that think there is no land, when they can see nothing but sea.

Sir Francis Bacon (1561-1626)
The Advancement of Learning

Like one that stands upon a promontory,
And spies a far-off shore where he would tread,
Wishing his foot were equal with his eye.

William Shakespeare (1564-1616)
King Henry the Sixth, Part II, Act 3, scene 2

Many voyages have been pretended, yet hitherto never any thoroughly accomplished by our nation, of exact discovery into the bowels of those main, ample, and vast countries extended infinitely into the north from thirty degrees, or rather from twenty-five degrees, of septentrional latitude, neither hath a right way been taken of planting a Christian habitation and regiment upon the same, as well may appear both by the little we yet do actually possess therein, and by our ignorance of the riches and secrets within those lands, which unto this day we know chiefly by the travel and report of other nations, and most of the French, who albeit they cannot challenge such right and interest unto the said countries as we, neither these many years have had opportunity nor means so great to discover and to plant, being vexed with the calamities of intestine wars, as we have had by the inestimable benefit of our long and happy peace, yet have they both ways performed more, and had long since attained a sure possession and settled government of many provinces in those northerly parts of America, if their many attempts into those foreign and remote lands had not been impeached by their garboils at home.

Edward Haies (c.1583)
Sir Humphrey Gilbert's Voyage to Newfoundland

If a man be gracious and courteous to strangers, it shows he is a citizen of the world.

Sir Francis Bacon (1561-1626)
'Of Goodness and Goodness of Nature', *Essays*

Home-keeping youths have ever homely wits.

William Shakespeare (1564-1616)
The Two Gentlemen of Verona, Act 1, scene 1

Oh my America, my new founde land,
My kingdome, safeliest when with one man
mann'd

John Donne (1572-1631)
'Elegie: On His Mistress Going to Bed'

I struck the Board and cried, No more:
I will abroad.
What? Shall I ever sigh and pine?
My lines and life are free, free as the road
Loose as the wind, as large as store.

George Herbert (1593-1633)
'The Collar'

Go in peace, to love and serve the Lord

The Book of Common Prayer 1662

A man should ever, as much as in him lieth, be ready booted to take his journey.

Michel de Montaigne (1533-1592)
Essays, Book I

Sweetest love, I do not goe,
For wearinesse of thee,
Nor in hope the world can show
A fitter Love for mee;
But since that I
Must dye at last, 'tis best,
To use my selfe in jest
Thus by fain'd deaths to dye;

Yesternight the Sunne went hence,
And yet is here to day,
He hath no desire nor sense,
Nor halfe so short a way.
Then feare not mee,
But beleeve that I shall make
Speedier journeyes, since I take
More wings and spurres then hee.

John Donne (1572-1631)
'Song'

What English shippes did heretofore ever anker in the mighty river of Plate? Passe and repasse the impassable (in former opinion) straight of Magellan, range along the coast of Chili, Peru, and all the backside of Nova Hispania, further than any Christian ever passed, traverse the mighty bredth of the South Seas, land upon the Luzones in despight of the enemy, enter into alliance, amity, and traffike with the princes of the Molluccas and the Isle of Java, double the famous Cape of Bona Speranza, arrive at the Isle of Santa Helena, and last of al returne home most richly laden with the commodities of China, as the subjects of this now flourishing monarchy have done?

Richard Hakluyt (1552-1616)
Dedication, *Discoveries of the World*

Every mile is two in winter.

George Herbert (1593-1633)
Jacula Prudentum

Travelling is almost like conversing with those from other centuries.

René Descartes (1596-1650)
Le Discours de la méthode, ch. 1

Absence, hear thou my protestation
Against thy strength, Distance, and length;
Do what thou canst for alteration:
For hearts of truest mettle
Absence doth join, and Time doth settle.

John Donne (1572-1631)
'Present in Absence'

I'll view the manners of the town,
Peruse the traders, gaze upon the buildings,
And then return and sleep within mine inn,
For with long travel I am stiff and weary.

William Shakespeare (1564-1616)
The Comedy of Errors, Act 1, scene 2

O how I long to travell back,
And tread again that ancient track!
That I might once more reach that plaine,
Where first I left my glorious traine,
From whence th' inlightened spirit sees
That shady City of palme trees

Henry Vaughan (1622-1695)
'The Retreate'

In what torne ship soever I embarke,
That ship shall be my embleme of thy Arke;
What sea soever swallow mee, that flood
Shall be to mee an embleme of thy blood;
Though thou with clouds of anger do disguise
Thy face; yet through that maske I know those eyes,
Which, though they turne away sometimes,
They never will despise.

John Donne (1572-1631)
'A Hymne to Christ, at the Authors last going into Germany'

I, who travel most often for my pleasure, do not direct myself so badly. If it looks ugly on the right, I take the left; if I find myself unfit to ride my horse, I stop...Have I left something unseen behind me? I go back; it is still on my road. I trace no fixed line, either straight or crooked.

Michel de Montaigne (1533-1592)
'Of Vanity', *The Essays*

A REPORT of the VOYAGE and success thereof, attempted in the year of our Lord 1583, by SIR HUMPHREY GILBERT, KNIGHT, with other gentlemen assisting him in that action, intended to discover and to plant Christian inhabitants in place convenient, upon those large and ample countries extended northward from the Cape of FLORIDA, lying under very temperate climes, esteemed fertile and rich in minerals, yet not in the actual possession of any Christian prince. Written by MR. EDWARD HAIES, gentleman, and principal actor in the same voyage, who alone continued unto the end, and, by God's special assistance, returned home with his retinue safe and entire

Edward Haies (c.1583)
Title page, *Sir Humphrey Gilbert's Voyage to Newfoundland*

I had rather have a fool to make me merry than experience to make me sad—and to travel for it too!

William Shakespeare (1564-1616)
As You Like It, Act 4, scene 1

Dromio: No longer from head to foot than from hip to hip: she is spherical, like a globe; I could find out countries in her.

Antipholus: In what part of her body stands Ireland?

Dromio: Marry, sir, in her buttocks: I found it out by the bogs.

Antipholus: Where Scotland?

Dromio: I found it by the barrenness; hard in the palm of the hand.

Antipholus: Where France?

Dromio: In her forehead; armed and reverted, making war against her heir.

Antipholus: Where England?

Dromio: I looked for the chalky cliffs, but I could find no whiteness in them: but I guess it stood in her chin, by the salt rheum that ran between France and it.

Antipholus: Where Spain?

Dromio: Faith, I saw not; but I felt it hot in her breath.

Antipholus: Where America, the Indies?

Dromio: O, sir! upon her nose, all o'er embellished with rubies, carbuncles, sapphires, declining their rich aspect to the hot breath of Spain, who sent whole armadoes of caracks to be ballast at her nose.

Antipholus: Where stood Belgia, the Netherlands?

Dromio: O, sir! I did not look so low.

William Shakespeare (1564-1616)
The Comedy of Errors, Act 3 scene 2

Though regions farr devided
And tedious tracts of tyme,
By my misfortune guided,
Make absence thought a cryme;
Though wee weare set a sunder
As far, as East from West,
Love still would worke this wonder,
Thou shouldst be in my breast.

Aurelian Towshend (c.1583-1681)
'Song'

Ferneze: Welcome, great Basso: how fares Calymath? What wind drives you thus into Malta road?

Basso: The wind that bloweth all the world beside. Desire of gold.

Christopher Marlowe (1564-1593)
The Jew of Malta, Act 3, scene 2

By a knight of ghosts and shadows
I summon'd am to a tourney
Ten leagues beyond the wide world's end:
Methinks it is no journey.

Unknown
Tom o' Bedlam's Song

Weary with toil, I haste me to my bed,
The dear repose for limbs with travel tired;
But then begins a journey in my head
To work my mind, when body's work's expired:

William Shakespeare (1564-1616)
'Weary with toil, I haste me to my bed'

I have undergone many constructions; I have been accompanied with many sorrows, with labour, hunger, heat, sickness, and peril; it appeareth, notwithstanding, that I made no other bravado of going to the sea, than was meant, and that I was never hidden in Cornwall, or elsewhere, as was supposed.

They have grossly belied me that forejudged that I would rather become a servant to the Spanish king than return; and the rest were much mistaken, who would have persuaded that I was too easeful and sensual to undertake a journey of so great travail. But if what I have done receive the gracious construction of a painful pilgrimage, and purchase the least remission, I shall think all too little, and that there were wanting to the rest many miseries. But if both the times past, the present, and what may be in the future, do all by one grain of gall continue in eternal distaste, I do not then know whether I should bewail myself, either for my too much travail and expense, or condemn myself for doing less than that which can deserve nothing. From myself I have deserved no thanks, for I am returned a beggar, and withered; but that I might have bettered my poor estate, it shall appear from the following discourse, if I had not only respected her Majesty's future honour and riches.

Sir Walter Ralegh (c.1552-1618)
Dedication, *The Discovery of Guiana*

Here take my Picture; though I bid farewell,
Thine, in my heart, where my soul dwels, shall dwell.
'Tis like me now, but I dead, 'twill be more
When we are shadowes both, then 'twas before.
When weather-beaten I come back; my hand,
Perhaps with rude oares torn, or Sun beams tann'd.
My face and brest of hairecloth, and my head
With cares rash soudaine hoarinesse o'rspread.
My body'a sack of bones, broken within,
And powder blew staines scatter'd on my skinne;
If rivall fools taxe thee to'have lov'd a man,
So foule, and coarse, as, Oh, I may seeme then,
This shall say what I was;

John Donne (1572-1631)
'Elegie: His Picture'

How heavy do I journey on the way
When what I seek, my weary travel's end,
Doth teach that ease and that repose to say,
'Thus far the miles are measur'd from thy friend!'

William Shakespeare (1564-1616)
Sonnet 50

I left the confines and the bounds of Afric,
And made a voyage into Europe,
Where, by the river Tyras, I subdu'd
Stoka, Podolia, and Codemia;
Then cross'd the sea and came to Oblia,
And Nigra Silva, where the devils dance,
Which, in spite of them, I set on fire.
From thence I cross'd the gulf call'd by the name
Mare Majore of the inhabitants.
Yet shall my soldiers make no period
Until Natolia kneel before your feet.

Christopher Marlowe (1564-1593)
Tamberlaine, Part II, Act 1, scene 6

The land is the finest for cultivation that I ever in my life set foot upon, and it also abounds in trees of every description. The natives are very good people; for when they saw that I would not remain, they supposed that I was afraid of their bows, and taking the arrows they broke them in pieces and threw them into the fire.

Henry Hudson (d.1611)
On first meeting the people of New York in 1609
Tales of Old New York

Go; and if that word have not quite killed thee,
Ease me with death, by bidding me go too.

John Donne (1572-1631)
'The Expiration'

Learned Faustus,
To find the secrets of astronomy,
Graven in the book of Jove's high firmament,
Did mount him up to scale Olympus top,
Where, sitting in a chariot burning bright,
Drawn by the strength of yoked dragons' necks,
He views the clouds, the planets and the stars,
The tropic, zones, and quarters of the sky,
From the bright circle of the horned moon,
Even to the height of the Primum Mobile.
And whirling round with this circumference,
Within the concave compass of the pole,
From east to west his dragons swiftly glide,
And in eight days did bring him home again.

Christopher Marlowe (1564-1593)
Doctor Faustus, Act 3, scene 1

Although my body is elsewhere, my heart is always here. Our Lord gave me the greatest grace ever awarded to anybody after David. The deeds of my enterprise already shine, and they would be even brighter if the obscurity of the government did not cover them.

Christopher Columbus (1451-1506)
Letter to the Bank of San Giorgio 1502, on leaving for his fourth voyage

Those new regions [America] which we have found and explored with the fleet...we may right call a New World... a contintent more densely peopled and abounding in animals than our Europe or Asia or Africa; and in addition, a climate milder than in any region known to us.

Amerigo Vespucci (1454-1512)
Letter called 'Mundus Novus' (1503) written to Lorenzo de Medici

I am rather inclined to believe that this is the land God gave to Cain.

Jacques Cartier (1491-1557)
On discovering the shore of the Gulf of St Lawrence
H P Biggar (ed) *The Voyages of Jacques Cartier*

You brave heroic minds
Worthy your country's name,
That honour still pursue;
Go and subdue! Whilst loitering hinds
Lurk here at home with shame.

Britons, you stay too long:
Quickly aboard bestow you,
And with a merry gale
Swell your stretch'd sail
With vows as strong
As the winds that blow you.

Your course securely steer,
West and by south forth keep!
Rocks, lee-shores, nor shoals
When Eolus scowls
You need not fear;
So absolute the deep.

And cheerfully at sea
Success you still entice
To get the pearl and gold,
And ours to hold
Virginia,
Earth's only paradise.

Michael Drayton (1563-1631)
'To the Virginian Voyage'

In ship, freight with rememberance
Of thoughts and pleasures past,
He sails that hath in governance
My life while it will last:
With scalding sighs, for lack of gale,
Furthering his hope, that is his sail,
Toward me, the swete port of his avail.

Henry Howard, Earl of Surrey (1517-1547)
'Complaint of the Absence of her Lover Being upon the Sea'

I am in blood
Stepped in so far that,
Should I wade no more,
Returning were as tedious as go o'er.

William Shakespeare (1564-1616)
Macbeth, Act 3, scene 4

The fifteenth day of November, in the year of our Lord 1577, Master Francis Drake, with a fleet of five ships and barks, and to the number of 164 men, gentlemen and sailors, departed from Plymouth, giving out his pretended voyage for Alexandria. But the wind falling contrary, he was forced the next morning to put into Falmouth

Haven, in Cornwall, where such and so terrible a tempest took us, as few men have seen the like, and was indeed so vehement that all our ships were like to have gone to wrack. But it pleased God to preserve us from that extremity, and to afflict us only for that present with these two particulars: the mast of our Admiral, which was the *Pelican*, was cut overboard for the safeguard of the ship, and the *Marigold* was driven ashore, and somewhat bruised. For the repairing of which damages we returned again to Plymouth; and having recovered those harms, and brought the ships again to good state, we set forth the second time from Plymouth, and set sail the thirteenth day of December following.

Francis Pretty (c.1579)
Sir Francis Drake's Famous Voyage Round the World

For I must go where lazy Peace,
Will hide her drouzy head;
And, for the sport of Kings, encrease
The numbers of the Dead.

Sir William Davenant (1606-1668)
'The Souldier going to the Field'

I am about to take my last voyage, a great leap into the dark.

Thomas Hobbes (1588-1679)
Last words

Absent from thee I languish still,
Then ask me not, when I return?
The straying Fool 'twill plainly kill,
To wish all Day, all Night to Mourn

John Wilmot, Earl of Rochester (1647-1680)
'A Song'

Being thus arrived in a good harbour, and brought safe to land, they fell upon their knees and blessed the God of heaven, who had brought them over the vast and furious ocean, and delivered them from all the perils and miseries thereof, again to set their feet on firm and stable earth, their proper element.

William Bradford (1590-1657)
Of Plymouth Plantation

Get thee to a nunnery, go, farewell. Or if thou wilt needs marry, marry a fool; for wise men know well enough what monsters you make of them. To a nunnery, go, and quickly too. Farewell.

William Shakespeare (1564-1616)
Hamlet, Act 3, scene 1

We carry with us the wonders we seek without us: There is all Africa and her prodigies in us.

Sir Thomas Browne (1605-1682)
Religio Medici

On Whitsunday Eve, being the 24th of May, in the year 1572, Captain DRAKE in the *Pascha of Plymouth* of 70 tons, his Admiral; with the *Swan* of the same port, of 25 tons, his vice-admiral, in which his brother JOHN DRAKE was Captain (having in both of them, of men and boys seventy-three, all voluntarily assembled; of which the eldest was fifty, all the rest under thirty: so divided that there were forty-seven in the one ship, and twenty-six in the other. Both richly furnished with victuals and apparel for a whole year; and no less heedfully provided of all manner of munition, artillery, artificers, stuff and tools, that were requisite for such a Man-of-war in such an attempt: but especially having three dainty pinnaces made in Plymouth, taken asunder all in pieces, and stowed aboard, to be set up as occasion served), set sail, from out of the Sound of Plymouth, with intent to land at Nombre de Dios.

Nephew of Sir Francis Drake (1588-1637)
Sir Francis Drake Revived

All places, all airs make unto me one country; I am in England, everywhere and under any meridian.

Sir Thomas Browne (1605-1682)
Religio Medici

Vices may be said to await us along the course of our lives like hosts with whom we lodge successively on a journey; and I doubt that experience would cause us to avoid them, if we could travel the same road twice.

François, Duc De La Rochefoucauld
(1613–1680)
Moral Maxims and Reflections, no. 192

...or, if some other place,
From your dominion won, the Ethereal King
Possesses lately, thither to arrive I travel this profound.
Direct my course; Directed, no mean recompense it brings
To your behoof, if I that region lost.

John Milton (1608-1674)
Paradise Lost, Book 2

The world in all doth but two nations bear –
The good, the bad; and these mixed everywhere.

Andrew Marvell (1621-1678)
'The Loyal Scot'

Hope, deceitful though it be, is at least of this good use to us - that while we are travelling through this life, it conducts us by an easier and more pleasant way to our journey's end.

François, Duc De La Rochefoucauld (1613-1680)
Moral Maxims and Reflections, no. 169

Say therefore on;
For I that day was absent, as befell,
Bound on a voyage uncouth and obscure,
Far on excursion toward the gates of Hell

John Milton (1608-1674)
Paradise Lost, Book 8

Some men forward motion love
But I by backward steps would move.

Henry Vaughan (1622-1695)
'The Retreat', *Silex Scintillans*

If to be absent were to be
Away from thee;
Or that when I am gone
You or I were alone;
Then, my Lucasta, might I crave
Pity from blustering wind, or swallowing wave.

Richard Lovelace (1618–1657)
'To Lucasta, Going Beyond the Sea'

In a calm sea, every man is a pilot

John Ray (1627-1705)
English Proverbs

Where the remote Bermudas ride
In th' Ocean's bosome unespy'd,
From a small Boat, that row'd along
The listning Winds receiv'd this song.

What should we do but sing his Praise
That led us through the watry Maze
Unto an Isle so long unknown,
And yet far kinder than our own,
Where he the huge Sea-Monsters wracks,
That lift the Deep upon their Backs ?

Andrew Marvell (1621-1678)
'Bermudas'

Void of strong desire and fear,
Life's wide ocean trust no more;
Strive thy little bark to steer
With the tide, but near the shore.

Thus prepared, thy shorten'd sail
Shall, when'er the winds increase,
Seizing each propitious gale,
Waft thee to the port of Peace.

George Bubb Dodington, Lord Melcombe
(c.1691-1762)
'Shorten Sail'

Fir'd at first Sight with what the Muse imparts,
In fearless Youth we tempt the height of Arts,
While from the bounded Level of our Mind,
Short views we take, nor see the Lengths behind,
But more advanc'd, behold with strange Suprize
New, distant Scenes of endless Science rise!
So pleas'd at first, the tow'ring Alps we try,
Mount o'er the Vales, and seem to tread the Sky,
Th'Eternal Snows appear already past,
And the first Clouds and Mountains seem the last:
But those attain'd, we tremble to survey
The growing Labours of the lengthen'd Way,
Th'increasing Prospect tires our wandring Eyes,
Hills peep o'er Hills, and Alps on Alps arise!

Alexander Pope (1688-1744)
'An Essay on Criticism'

Never was woman better us'd in this World, that went upon no other Account than I did; I had three Women-Servants to wait on me, one whereof was an old Madam –, who thorowly understood her Business, and manag'd every thing, as if she had been Major Domo; so I had no Trouble; they had one Coach to themselves, and the Prince and I in the other; only that sometimes, where he knew it necessary, I went into their Coach; and one particular Gentleman of the Retinue rode with him.

I shall say no more of the Journey, than that when we came to those frightful Mountains, the Alps; there was no travelling in our Coaches, so he order'd a Horse-Litter, but carried by Mules, to be provided for me, and himself went on Horseback; the Coaches went some other Way back to Lyons; then we had coaches hir'd at Turin, which met us at Susa; so that we were accommodated again, and went by easie Journeys afterwards, to Rome, where his Business, whatever it was, call'd him to stay some time; and from thence to Venice.

Daniel Defoe (1660-1731)
Roxana

As I walked through the wilderness of this world

John Bunyan (1628-1688)
The Pilgrim's Progress

And so to bed

Samuel Pepys (1633-1703)
Diary, 20 April 1660

Ulysses travel'd; so did Æneas: but neither of them were the first travellers; for Cain went into the land of Nod before they were born

John Dryden (1631-1700)
Dedication, *The Aenead*

And did those feet in ancient time
Walk upon England's mountains green?
And was the holy Lamb of God
On England's pleasant pastures seen?

William Blake (1757-1827)
Preface from *Milton*

Then he thanked Mr Great-heart, for his conduct and kindness, and so addressed himself to his journey. When he came at the brink of the River, he said, 'Now I shall have no more need of these crutches, since yonder are chariots and horses for me to ride on.' The last words he was heard to say, was, 'Welcome life.' So he went his way.

John Bunyan (1628-1688)
The Pilgrim's Progress

My father, a wise and grave man, gave me serious and excellent counsel against what he foresaw was my design...He asked me what reasons more than a meer wandering inclination I had for leaving my father's house and my native country, where I might be well introduced, and had a prospect of raising my fortune by application and industry, with a life of ease and pleasure. He told me it was for men of desperate fortunes on one hand, or of aspiring, superior fortune on the other, who went abroad upon adventures, to rise by enterprize, and make themselves famous in undertakings of a nature out of the common road.

Daniel Defoe (1660-1731)
Robinson Crusoe

I am weary of travelling and am resolved to go abroad no more. But when I am dead and gone I know not what my brother will do: I am much afraid that when he comes to wear the crown he will be obliged to travel again.

King Charles II (1630-1685)
Attributed

Paris is, indeed, a place very different from the Hebrides, but it is to a hasty traveller not so fertile of novelty, nor affords so many opportunities of remark.

Samuel Johnson (1709-1784)
Letter to James Boswell, 16 November, 1775

Faith, sir, we are here today and gone tomorrow.

Aphra Benn (1640-1689)
The Lucky Chance, Act 4

And now there came both mist and snow,
And it grew wondrous cold:
And ice, mast-high, came floating by,
As green as emerald.

And through the drifts the snowy clifts
Did send a dismal sheen:
Nor shapes of men nor beasts we ken—
The ice was all between.

The ice was here, the ice was there,
The ice was all around:
It crack'd and growl'd, and roar'd and howl'd,
Like noises in a swound!

Samuel Taylor Coleridge (1772-1834)
'The Rime of the Ancient Mariner'

A daring pilot in extremity;
Pleased with danger, when the waves went high,
He sought the storms; but, for a calm unfit,
Would steer to nigh the sands, to boast his wit.

John Dryden (1631-1700)
Absolem and Achitophel

September 30, 1659. I, poor miserable Robinson Crusoe, being shipwrecked, during a dreadful storm, in the offing, came on shire on this dismal and unfortunate island, which I called the Island of Despair, all the rest of the ship's company being drowned, and my self almost dead.

Daniel Defoe (1660-1731)
Robinson Crusoe

Happy is the man whose wish and care
A few paternal acres bound,
Content to breathe his native air,
In his own ground.

Alexander Pope (1688-1744)
'Ode on Solitude'

Every body continues in its state of rest, or of uniform motion in a right line, unless it is compelled to change that state by the forces impressed upon it.

Sir Isaac Newton (1642-1727)
Principa Mathematica, Laws of Motion 1

Like pilgrims to th'appointed place we tend;
The world's an inn, and death the journey's end.

John Dryden (1631-1700)
Palamon and Arcite, Book 3

Westward the course of empire takes its way

George Berkeley (1685-1753)
'On the Prospect of Planting Arts and Learning in America'

If with me you'd fondly stray
Over the hills and far away

John Gay (1685-1732)
The Beggar's Opera

If you be wise, go not far to dine;
You'll spend in coach hire more than save in wine.

Jonathan Swift (1667-1745)
'A Description of a City Shower'

The change of motion is proportional to the motive force impressed; and is made in the direction of the right line in which that force is impressed.

Sir Isaac Newton (1642-1727)
Principa Mathematica, Laws of Motion 2

The months and days are the travellers of eternity. The years that come and go are also voyagers.

Bash (1644-1694)
The Narrow Road of Oku

I began this desperate voyage on February 15, 1714, at 9 o'clock in the morning. The wind was very favourable; however, I made use at first only of my paddles; but considering I should soon be weary, and that the wind might probably chop about, I ventured to set up my little sail, and thus, with the help of the tide, I went at the rate of a league and a half an hour, as near as I could guess. My master and his friends continued on the shore, till I was almost out of sight; and I often heard the sorrel nag (who always loved me) crying out, 'Hnuy killa nyha maiah Yahoo' ('Take care of thyself, gentle Yahoo').

Jonathan Swift (1667-1745)
Gulliver's Travels, Part 4, ch. 2

'Twas for the good of my country that I should be abroad.

George Farquhar (1678-1707)
The Beaux Strategem, Act III

The use of travelling is to regulate imagination by reality, and instead of thinking how things may be, to see them as they are.

Samuel Johnson (1709-1784)
Mrs Piozzi's Anecdotes of Samuel Johnson

The first step is the hardest

Marquise du Deffand (1699-1780)
Letter to d'Alembert, 1763

As the Spanish proverb says 'He who would bring home the wealth of the Indies must carry the wealth of the Indies with him.' So it is in travelling, a man must carry knowledge with him if he would bring home knowledge.

Samuel Johnson (1709-1784)
from *James Boswell, Life of Johnson*

The coast of France was sighted at last.
'Have you ever been to France, Sir?' asked Candide.

'Yes,' said Martin, 'I have travelled in several provinces. In some you find half the people are fools, and in others you find them much too subtle. There are some parts of the country where people are simple and stupid, and others where they pretend to be witty. But wherever you go in France, you will find their three chief preoccupations are making love, backbiting, and talking nonsense.'

Voltaire (1694-1778)
Candide

Fools rush in where angels fear to tread.

Alexander Pope (1688-1744)
'An Essay on Criticism'

When Britain first at Heaven's command
Arose from out the azure main,
This was the charter of the land,
And guardian angels sung this strain:
Rule, Britannia, rule the waves
Britons never will be slaves.

James Thomson (1700-1748)
Rule, Britannia, rule the waves; *Alfred: A Masque*, Act 2

Ladybird, ladybird,
Fly away home,
Your house is on fire
And your children are all gone

Tommy Thumb's Pretty Song book (1744)

I always love to begin a journey on Sundays because I shall have the prayers of the Church, to preserve all that travel by land, or by water.

Jonathan Swift (1667-1745)
Polite Conversation

Being in a ship is being in jail, with the chance of being drowned.

Samuel Johnson (1709-1784)
from *James Boswell, Life of Johnson*

I pity the man who can travel from Dan to Beersheba and cry 'tis all barren - and so it is; and so is all the world to him who will not cultivate the fruits it offers.

Laurence Sterne (1713-1768)
A Sentimental Journey

Come, O thou Traveller unknown,
Whom still I hold, but cannot see

Charles Wesley (1707-1788)
'Wrestling Jacob', *Hymns and Sacred Poems*

To Contemplation's sober eye
Such is the race of Man:
And they that creep and they that fly,
Shall end where they began.

Thomas Grey (1716-1771)
'Ode on the Spring'

The noblest prospect which a Scotsman ever sees is the high road that leads him to England.

Samuel Johnson (1709-1784)
from *James Boswell, Life of Johnson*

Now hang it! quoth I as I look'd towards the French coast – A man should know something of his own country too, before he goes abroad.

Laurence Sterne (1713-1768)
The Life and Opinions of Tristram Shandy

Nature is the nurse of sentiment – the true source of taste – yet what misery, as well as rapture, is produced by a quick perception of the beautiful and sublime, when it is exercised in observing animated nature, when every beauteous feeling and emotion excited responsive sympathy, and the harmonised soul sinks into melancholy, or rises to extasy, just as the chords are touched, like the aeolian harp agitated by the changing wind.

Mary Wollstonecraft (1759-1797)
Letters Written during a Short Rresidence in Norway, Sweden and Denmark

There is nothing which has yet been contrived by man by which so much happiness is produced as by a good tavern or inn.

Samuel Johnson (1709-1784)
from *James Boswell, Life of Johnson*

There is no ordinary Part of humane Life which expresseth so much a good Mind, and a right inward Man, as his Behaviour upon Meeting with Strangers, especially such as may seem the most unsuitable Companions to him: Such a Man when he falleth in the Way with Persons of Simplicity and Innocence, however knowing he may be in the Ways of Men, will not vaunt himself thereof; but will the rather hide his Superiority to them, that he may not be painful unto them.

Richard Steele (1672-1729)
The Spectator, no 132

This same philosophy is a good horse in the stable, but an arrant jade on a journey.

Oliver Goldsmith (1730-1774)
The Good-Natured Man, Act 1

Alone, alone, all, all alone,
Alone on a wide wide sea!
And never a saint took pity on
My soul in agony.

Samuel Taylor Coleridge (1772-1834)
'The Rime of the Ancient Mariner'

A traveller, to thee unknown,
Is he that calls, a warrior's son.
Thou the deeds of light shalt know;
Tell me what is done below,
From whom yon glitt'ring board is spread,
Drest for whom yon golden bed.

Thomas Grey (1716-1771)
'The Descent of Odin'

So as to comprehend that the sky is blue everywhere one doesn't need to travel around the world.

Johann Wolfgang von Goethe (1749-1832)
Wilhelm Meister's Travels

I am willing to love all mankind, except an American.

Samuel Johnson (1709-1784)
from *James Boswell, Life of Johnson*

Every nation...have their refinements and *grossiertés*...There is a balance...of good and bad every where; and nothing but the knowing it is so can emancipate one half of the world from the prepossessions which it holds against the other—that [was] the advantage of travel...it taught us mutual toleration; and mutual toleration...taught us mutual love.

Laurence Sterne (1713-1768)
A Sentimental Journey

As the Norwegians do not frequently see travellers, they are very curious to know their business, and who they are – so curious that I was half tempted to adopt Dr Franklin's plan, when travelling in America, where they are equally prying, which was to write on a paper for public inspection, my name, from whence I came, where I was going, and what was my business. But if I were importuned by their curiosity, their friendly gestures gratified me. A woman, coming alone, interested them. And I know not whether my weariness gave me a look of peculiar delicacy; but they approached to assist me, and enquire after my wants, as if they were afraid to hurt, and wished to protect me.

Mary Wollstonecraft (1759-1797)
Letters Written during a Short Residence in Norway, Sweden and Denmark

Ah, Sun-flower, weary of time,
Who countest the steps of the Sun,
Seeking after that sweet golden clime
Where the traveller's journey is done:
Where the Youth pined away with desire,
And the pale Virgin shrouded in snow
Arise from their graves, and aspire
Where my Sun-flower wishes to go.

William Blake (1757-1827)
'Ah! Sun-flower', *Songs of Experience*

Travelling is the ruin of all happiness! There's no looking at a building here after seeing Italy.

Fanny Burney (1752-1840)
Cecilia

In Xanadu did Kubla Khan
A stately pleasure-dome decree:
Where Alph, the sacred river, ran
Through caverns measureless to man
Down to a sunless sea.

Samuel Taylor Coleridge (1722-1834)
Kubla Khan

Well, the wedding is over, the good folks are joined for better for worse—a shocking clause that!—'tis preparing one to lead a long journey, and to know the path is not altogether strewed with roses.

Fanny Burney (1752-1840)
Diary, May 15, 1769

I wander thro' each charter'd street
Near where the charter'd Thames does flow,
And mark in every face I meet
Marks of weakness, marks of woe.

William Blake (1757-1827)
'London', *Songs of Innocence and Experience*

An English man does not travel to see English men.

Laurence Sterne (1713-1768)
A Sentimental Journey

Goosey goosey gander,
Wither shall I wander?
Upstairs, downstairs,
In my lady's chamber.

Gammer Gurton's Garland, 1784

Over all the mountain tops is peace.

Johan Wolfgang von Goethe (1749-1832)
Wanderers Nachtleid

Oh, London is a fine town
A very famous city,
Where the streets are paved with gold,
And all the maidens pretty.

George Colman the Younger (1762-1836)
The Heir at Law, Act 1, scene 2

O mirk, mirk is this midnight hour,
And loud the tempest's roar;
A waefu' wanderer seeks thy tower,
Lord Gregory, ope thy door.
An exile frae her father's ha',
And a' for loving thee;
At least some pity on me shaw,
If love it may na be.

Robert Burns (1759-1796)
'Lord Gregory: A Ballad'

I travel'd thro' a Land of Men,
A Land of Men & Women too,
And heard & saw such dreadful things
As cold Earth wanderers never knew.

William Blake (1757-1827)
'The Mental Traveller', *Songs of Innocence and Experience*

By late 1778 the great trail stretching from Cumberland gap to the Ohio was becoming well-worn by the treading of ambitious families on their way to build new homes and to found a new society.

Travellers and foreign land-hunters found the roads filled with poor souls moving westwards... These were spirited travellers, however, and the burden of trials and hardships sat lightly upon them; they possessed at all times a sense of humour.

Thomas D Clarke
The Rampaging Frontier (1939)

Pussy cat, pussy cat, where have you been?
I've been to London to look at the queen.

Traditional nursery rhyme

Soon as she was gone from me,
A traveller came by
Silently, invisibly:
He took her with a sigh

William Blake (1757-1827)
'Never seek to tell thy Love'

I seemed every night to descend, not metaphorically, but literally to descend, into chasms and sunless abysses, depths below depths, from which it seemed hopeless that I could ever reascend.

Thomas de Quincy (1785-1859)
Confessions of an English Opium Eater

There is no doubt that an english winter would put an end to me, and do so in a lingering and hateful manner, therefore I must either voyage or journey to Italy as a soldier marches up to a battery. My nerves at present are the worst part of me, yet they feel soothed when I think that come what may, I shall not be destined to remain in one spot long enough to take hatred of any four particular bed-posts.

John Keats (1795-1821)
Letter to Percy Bysshe Shelley, August 16, 1820

'Tis thus with people in an open boat,
They live upon the love of live, and bear
More than can be believed, or even thought,
And stand like rocks the tempest's wear and tear;
And hardship still has been the sailor's lot,
Since Noah's ark went cruising here and there;

She had a curious crew as well as cargo.
Like the first old Greek privateer, the Argo.

Lord Byron (1788-1824)
Don Juan, Canto II, 66

Catherine looked round and saw Miss Tilney leaning on her brother's arm, walking slowly down the street. She saw them both looking back at her. 'Stop, stop, Mr Thorpe,' she impatiently cried, 'It is Miss Tilney; it is indeed. – How could you tell me they were gone? – Stop, stop, I will get out this moment and go to them.' But to what purpose did she speak? – Thorpe only lashed his horse into a brisker trot; the Tilneys, who had soon ceased to look after her, were in a moment out of sight round the corner of Laura-place, and in another moment she was herself whisked into the Market-place. Still, however, and during the length of another street, she intreated him to stop. 'Pray, pray stop, Mr Thorpe. – I cannot go on. – I will not go on. – I must go back to Miss Tilney.' But Mr Thorpe only laughed, smacked his whip, encouraged his horse, made odd noises, and drove on.

Jane Austen (1775-1817)
Northanger Abbey, ch. 11

I travelled among unknown men,
In lands beyond the sea;
Nor England! did I know till then
What love I bore to thee.

William Wordsworth (1770-1850)
'I travelled among Unknown Men'

It's no fish ye're buying, it's men's lives.

Sir Walter Scott (1771-1832)
The Antiquary, ch. 11

A boat of rare device, which had no sail
But its own curvèd prow of thin moonstone,
Wrought like a web of texture fine and frail,
To catch those gentlest winds which are not known
To breathe, but by the steady speed alone
With which it cleaves the sparkling sea; and now
We are embarked – the mountains hang and frown
Over the starry deep that gleams below
A vast and dim expanse, as o'er the waves we go.

Percy Bysshe Shelley (1792-1822)
The Revolt of Islam, Canto 1

Tiber, the road which is spread by nature's own hand, threading her continent, was at my feet, and many a boat was tethered to the banks. I would with a few books, provisions, and my dog, embark in one of these and float down the current of the stream into the sea; and then, keeping near land, I would coast the beauteous shores and sunny promontories of the blue Mediterranean, pass Naples, along Calabria, and would dare the twin perils of Scylla and Charybdis; then, with fearless aim, (for what had I to lose?) skim ocean's surface towards Malta and the further Cyclades. I would avoid Constantinople, the sight of whose well-known towers and inlets belonged to another state of existence from my present one; I would coast Asia Minor, and Syria, and, passing the seven-mouthed Nile, steer northward again, till losing sight of forgotten Carthage and deserted Lybia, I should reach the pillars of Hercules. And then – no matter where – the oozy caves, and soundless depths of ocean may be my dwelling, before I accomplish this long-drawn voyage, or the arrow of disease find my heart as I float singly on the weltering Mediterranean; or, in some place I touch at, I may find what I seek – a companion; or if this may not be – to endless time, decrepit and grey headed – youth already in the grave with those I love – the lone wanderer will still unfurl his sail, and clasp the tiller – and, still obeying the breezes of heaven, forever round another and another promontory, anchoring in another and another bay, still ploughing seedless ocean, leaving behind the verdant land of native Europe, adown the tawny shore of Africa, having weathered the fierce seas of the Cape, I may moor my worn skiff in a creek, shaded by spicy groves of the odorous islands of the far Indian ocean.

Mary Shelley (1797-1851)
The Last Man, ch. 30

Give me the clear sky over my head, and the green turf beneath my feet, a winding road before me, and a three hours' march to dinner – and then to thinking!

William Hazlitt (1778-1830)
Table Talk

Much have I travell'd in the realms of gold,
And many goodly states and kingdoms seen;
Round many western islands have I been
Which bards in fealty to Apollo hold.

John Keats (1795-1821)
'On first looking into Chapman's Homer'

See Naples and die

Proverb

Adieu! adieu! my native shore
Fades o'er the waters blue...

Lord Byron (1788-1824)
Childe Harold's Pilgrimage, Canto I, stanza 13

There was too much wind to make the high part of the new Cobb pleasant for the ladies, and they agreed to get down the steps to the lower, and all were contented to pass quietly and carefully down the steep flight, excepting Louisa; she must be jumped down them by Captain Wentworth. In all their walks he had had to jump her from the stiles; the sensation was delightful to her. The hardness of the pavement for her feet, made him less willing upon the present occasion; he did it, however; she was safely down, and instantly, to shew her enjoyment, ran up the steps to be jumped down again...he put out his hands; she was too precipitate by half a second, she fell on the pavement on the Lower Cobb and was taken up lifeless!

Jane Austen (1775-1817)
Persuasion, ch. 12

But 'midst the crowd, the hum, the shock of men,
To hear, to see, to feel, and to possess,
And roam along, the world's tired denizen,
With none who bless us, none whom we can bless.

Lord Byron (1788-1824)
Childe Harold's Pilgrimage, Canto II. stanza 26

I wandered lonely as a cloud
That floats on high o'er vales and hills,
When all at once I saw a crowd,
A host, of golden daffodils;

William Wordsworth (1770-1850)
'I Wandered Lonely as a Cloud'

The party had landed on the border of a region that is, even to this day, less known to the inhabitants of the states than the deserts of Arabia, or the steppes of Tartary. It was the sterile and rugged district which separates the tributaries of Champlain from those of the Hudson, the Mohawk, and of the St Lawrence. Since the period of our tale, the active spirit of the country has surrounded it with a belt of rich and thriving settlements, though none but the hunter or the savage is ever known, even now, to penetrate its rude and wild recesses.

As Hawk-eye and the Mohicans had, however, often traversed the mountains and valleys of this vast wilderness, they did not hesitate to plunge into its depths with the freedom of men accustomed to its privations and difficulties. For many hours the travellers toiled on their laborious ways, guided by a star, or following the direction of some water-course, until the scout called a halt, and holding a short consultation with the Indians, they lighted their fire and made the usual preparations to pass the remainder of the night where they were.

James Fenimore Cooper (1789-1851)
The Last of the Mohicans, ch. 20

For many days,
Has he been wandering in uncertain ways:
Through wilderness, and woods of mossed oaks;
Counting his woe-worn minutes, by the strokes
Of the lone woodcutter; and listening still,
Hour after hour, to each lush-leav'd rill.

Till, weary, he sat down before the maw
Of a wide outlet, fathomless and dim
To wild uncertainty and shadows grim.
There, when new wonders ceas'd to float before,

And thoughts of self came on, how crude and sore
The journey homeward to habitual self!
A mad-pursuing of the fog-born elf,
Whose flitting lantern, through rude nettle-briar,
Cheats us into a swamp, into a fire,
Into the bosom of a hated thing.

John Keats (1795-1821)
Endymion, Book 2

They had a very fine day for Box Hill; and all the other outward circumstances of arrangement, accommodation, and punctuality, were in favour of a pleasant party. Mr Weston directed the whole, officiating safely between Hartfield and the vicarage, and every body was in good time. Emma and Harriet went together; Miss Bates and her niece, with the Eltons; the gentlemen on horseback. Mrs Weston remained with Mr Woodhouse. Nothing was wanting but to be happy when they got there. Seven miles were travelled in expectation of enjoyment, and every body had a burst of admiration on first arriving; but in the general amount of the day there was a deficiency. There was a langour, a want of spirits, a want of union, which could not be got over.

Jane Austen (1775-1817)
Emma, ch. 43

People commonly travel the world over to see rivers and mountains, new stars, garish birds, freak fish, grotesque breeds of human; they fall into an animal stupor that gapes at existence and they think they have seen something.

Soren Kierkegaard (1813-1855)
Fear and Trembling

I pursued him: and for many months this has been my task. Guided by a slight clue, I followed the windings of the Rhône, but vainly. The blue Mediterranean appeared, and by a strange chance, I saw the fiend enter by night and hide himself in a vessel bound for the Black Sea. I took my passage in the same ship, but he escaped, I know not how.

Amidst the wilds of Tartary and Russia, although he still evaded me, I have ever followed in his track. Sometime the peasants, scared by this horrid apparition, informed me of his path; sometimes he himself, who feared that if I lost all trace of him I should despair and die, left some mark to guide me. The snows descended on my head, and I saw the print of his huge step on the white plain.

Mary Shelley (1797-1851)
Frankenstein, ch. 24

When early youth had passed, he left
His cold fireside and alienated home
To seek strange truths in undiscovered lands.

Percy Bysshe Shelley (1792-1822)
Alastor; or the Spirit of Solitude

How many miles to Babylon?
Threescore miles and ten.
Can I get there by candlelight?
Yes, and back again.

Songs for the Nursery, 1805

He had travelled 'mongst the Arabs, Turks, and
Franks,
And knew the self-loves of the different nations;
And having lived with people of all ranks,
Had something ready upon most occasions –
Which got him a few presents and some thanks.
He varied with some skill his adulations;
To 'do at Rome as Romans do' a piece
Of conduct was which he observed in Greece.

Lord Byron (1788-1824)
Don Juan, Canto 3, LXXX1V

Early in the morning they were again mounted, and on the road to Edinburgh, though the pallid visages of some of the troop betrayed that they had spent a night of sleepless debauchery. They halted at Linlithgow, distinguished by its ancient palace, which Sixty Years since, was entire and habitable, and whose venerable ruins, not quite Sixty Years since, very narrowly escaped the unworthy fate of being converted into a barrack for French prisoners...

As they approached the metropolis of Scotland, through a champaign and cultivated country, the sounds of war began to be heard. The distant, yet distinct report of heavy cannon, fired at intervals, apprized Waverley that the work of destruction was going forward. Evan Balmawhapple seemed moved to take some precautions, by sending an advanced party in front of his troop, keeping the main body in tolerable order, and moving steadily forward.

Marching in this manner they speedily reached an eminence, from which they could view Edinburgh, stretching along the ridgy hill which slopes eastward from the Castle.

Sir Walter Scott (1771-1832)
Waverley, ch. 39

China? There lies a sleeping giant. Let him sleep! For when he wakes he will move the world.

Napoleon Bonaparte (1769-1821)
Attributed

In Naples the insolence of the mercenary fraternity has attained to such an unexampled pitch that the traveller is often tempted to doubt whether such a thing as honesty is known.

Karl Baedecker (1801-1859)
Guide to Southern Italy

What should I have known or written had I been a quiet, mercantile politician or a lord in waiting? A man must travel, and turmoil, or there is no existence.

Lord Byron (1788-1824)
Letter to poet Thomas Moore, August 31, 1820

The soul of a journey is liberty, perfect liberty, to think, feel, do just as one pleases.

William Hazlitt (1778-1830)
'On Going a Journey', *Table Talk*

Though the most beautiful creature were waiting for me at the end of a journey or a walk; though the carpet were of silk, the curtains of the morning clouds; the chairs and sofa stuffed with cygnet's down; the food manna, the wine beyond claret, the window opening on Winander Mere, I should not feel—or rather my happiness would not be so fine, as my solitude is sublime.

John Keats (1795-1821)
Letter, October 14-31, 1818

Summer was already past its prime, when Edgar reluctantly yielded his assent to their entreaties, and Catherine and I set out on our first ride to join her cousin. It was a close, sultry day: devoid of sunshine, but with a sky too dappled and hazy to threaten rain; and our place of meeting had been fixed at the guidestone, by the cross-roads. On arriving there, however, a little herd-boy, despatched as a messenger, told us that—

'Maister Linton wer just o' this side th' Heights: and he'd be mitch obleeged to us to gang on a bit further.'

'Then Master Linton has forgot the first injunction of his uncle,' I observed: 'he bid us keep on the Grange land, and here we are off at once.'

'Well, we'll turn our horses' heads round, when we reach him,' answered my companion, 'our excursion shall lie towards home.'

But when we reached him, and that was scarcely a quarter of a mile from his own door, we found he had no horse; and we were forced to dismount, and leave ours to graze. He lay on the heath, awaiting our approach, and did not rise till we came within a few yards. Then he walked so feebly, and looked so pale, that I immediately exclaimed—

'Why, Master Heathcliff, you are not fit for enjoying a ramble, this morning. How ill you do look!'

Emily Brontë (1818-1848)
Wuthering Heights ch. 26

There is a good deal of unmapped country within us which would have to be taken into account in an explanation of our gusts and storms.

George Eliot (1819-1880)
Daniel Deronda

The train swept us on:
Was this my father's England? the great isle?
The ground seemed cut up from the fellowship
Of verdure, field from field, as man from man;
The skies themselves looked low and positive,
As almost you could touch them with a hand,
And dared to do it they were so far off
From God's celestial crystals; all things blurred
And dull and vague.

Elizabeth Barrett Browning (1806-1861)
Aurora Leigh, Book 1

It was the subject of my perpetual dreams to render Paris the real capital of Europe. I sometimes wished it, for instance, to become a city with a population of two, three, or four millions – in a word, something fabulous, colossal, unexampled, until our days, and with public establishments suitable to its population.

Napoleon Bonaparte (1769-1821)
Comte de Las Cases, *Journal at St Helena*
4, August, 1816

As soon as they entered the copse, Lady Catherine began in the following manner:— 'You can be at no loss, Miss Bennet, to understand the reason of my journey hither. Your own heart, your own conscience, must tell you why I come.' Elizabeth looked with unaffected astonishment. 'Indeed, you are mistaken, madam; I have not been at all able to account for the honour of seeing you here.'

'Miss Bennet,' replied her Ladyship, in an angry tone, 'you ought to know that I am not to be trifled with. But however insincere you may choose to be, you shall not find me so. My character has ever been celebrated for its sincerity and frankness; and in a cause of such moment as this, I shall certainly not depart from it. A report of a most alarming nature reached me two days ago. I was told, that not only your sister was on the point of being most advantageously married, but that you, that Miss Elizabeth Bennet would, in all likelihood, be soon afterwards united to my nephew, my own nephew, Mr Darcy. Though I know it must be a scandalous falsehood, though I would not injure him so much as to suppose the truth of it possible, I instantly resolved on setting off for this place, that I might make my sentiments known to you.'

'If you believed it impossible to be true,' said Elizabeth, colouring with astonishment and disdain, 'I wonder you took the trouble of coming so far. What could your Ladyship propose by it?'

Jane Austen (1775-1817)
Pride and Prejudice, ch. 56

'Abroad', that large home of ruined reputations

George Eliot (1819-1880)
Felix Holt

Come, dear children, let us away;
Down and away below!
Now my brothers call from the bay,
Now the great winds shoreward blow,
Now the salt tides seaward flow;
Now the wild white horses play,
Champ and chafe and toss in the spray.
Children dear, let us away!
This way, this way!

Matthew Arnold (1822-1888)
'The Forsaken Merman'

What would the world be, once bereft
Of wet, and wilderness? Let them be left,
Oh, let them be left, wildness and wet;
Long live the weeds and the wilderness yet.

Gerard Manley Hopkins (1844-1889)
'Inversnaid'

What visions of glory would have broken upon his mind could he have known that he had indeed discovered a new continent, equal to the whole of the Old World in magnitude, and separated by two vast oceans from all the earth hitherto known by civilized man! And how would his magnanimous spirit have been consoled, amid the afflictions of age and the cares of penury, the neglect of a fickle public and the injustice of an ungrateful king, could he have anticipated the splendid empires which were to spread over the beautiful world he had discovered; and the nations, and tongues, and languages which were to fill its lands with his renown, and revere and bless his name to the latest posterity.

Washington Irving (1783-1859)
Life and Voyages of Christopher Columbus

The Owl and the Pussy-cat went to sea
In a beautiful pea-green boat,
They took some honey, and plenty of money,
Wrapped up in a five-pound note.

Edward Lear (1812-1888)
'The Owl and the Pussy Cat'

I wished to acquire the simplicity, native feelings, and virtues of savage life; to divest myself of the factitious habits, prejudices and imperfections of civilisation;...and to find, amidst the solitude and grandeur of the western wilds, more correct views of human nature and of the true interests of man. The season of snows was preferred, that I might experience the pleasure of suffering, and the novelty of danger.

Estwick Evans (1787-1866)
A Pedestrious Tour, of Four Thousand Miles, Through the Western States and Territories, During the Winter and Spring of 1818

Down, down, down. Would the fall never come to an end! 'I wonder how many miles I've fallen by this time?' she said aloud. 'I must be getting somewhere near the centre of the earth. Let me see: that would be four thousand miles down, I think—' (for, you see, Alice had learnt several things of this sort in her lessons in the schoolroom, and though this was not a very good opportunity for showing off her knowledge, as there was no one to listen to her, still it was good practice to say it over) '—yes, that's about the right distance – but then I wonder what Latitude or Longitude I've got to?' (Alice had no idea what Latitude was, or Longitude either, but thought they were nice grand words to say).

Lewis Carroll (1832-1898)
Alice's Adventures in Wonderland, ch.1

The sea is calm tonight.
The tide is full, the moon lies fair
Upon the straits - on the French coast the light
Gleams and is gone; the cliffs of England stand,
Glimmering and vast, out in the tranquil bay.

Matthew Arnold (1822-1888)
'Dover Beach'

America had often been discovered before Columbus, but it had always been hushed up.

Oscar Wilde (1854-1900)

Phileas Fogg had won his wager, and had made his journey around the world in eighty days. To do this he had employed every means of conveyance – steamers, railways, carriages, yachts, trading-vessels, sledges, elephants. The eccentric gentleman had throughout displayed all his marvellous qualities of coolness and exactitude. But what then? What had he really gained by all this trouble? What had he brought back from this long and weary journey?

Nothing, say you? Perhaps so; nothing but a charming woman, who, strange as it may appear, made him the happiest of men!

Truly, would you not for less than that make the tour around the world?

Jules Verne (1828-1905)
Around the World in 80 Days

I rose and endeavoured to unhasp the casement. The hook was soldered into the staple: a circumstance observed by me when awake, but forgotten. 'I must stop it, nevertheless!' I muttered, knocking my knuckles through the glass, and stretching an arm out to seize the importunate branch; instead of which, my fingers closed on the fingers of a little, ice-cold hand!

The intense horror of nightmare came over me: I tried to draw back my arm, but the hand clung to it, and a most melancholy voice sobbed, 'Let me in—let me in!' 'Who are you?' I asked, struggling, meanwhile, to disengage myself. 'Catherine Linton,' it replied, shiveringly (why did I think of Linton? I had read Earnshaw twenty times for Linton); 'I'm come home: I lost my way on the moor!'

Emily Brontë (1818-1848)
Wuthering Heights, ch. 3

Faster than fairies, faster than witches,
Bridges and houses, hedges and ditches;
And charging along like troops in a battle,
All through the meadows the horses and cattle:
All of the sights of the hill and the plain,
Fly as thick as driving rain;
And ever again, in the wink of an eye,
Painted stations whistle by.

Robert Louis Stevenson (1850-1894)
'From a Railway Carriage', *A Child's Garden of Verses*

I showed my appreciation of my native land in the usual Irish way by getting out of it as soon as I possibly could.

George Bernard Shaw (1856-1950)

For my part, I travel not to go anywhere, but to go. I travel for travel's sake. The great affair is to move.

Robert Louis Stevenson (1850-1894)
Travels with a Donkey

In the long winter evenings Pa talked to Ma about the Western country. In the west, the land was level, and there were no trees. The grass grew thick and high. There, the wild animals wandered and fed as though they were in a pasture that stretched much farther than a man could see, and there no settlers. Only Indians lived there.

Laura Ingalls Wilder (1867-1957)
Little House on the Prairie

Anywhere! Anywhere! So long as it is out of the world!

Charles Baudelaire (1821-1867)
Attributed

A traveller, by the faithful hound,
Half-buried in the snow was found.

Henry Wadsworth Longfellow (1807-1882)
'Excelsior'

But all I could think of, in the darkness and the cold,
was that I was leaving home and my folks were growing old.

Robert Louis Stevenson (1850-1894)
'Christmas at Sea', *Ballads*

They had come in the covered wagon all the long way from the Big Woods in Wisconsin, across Minnesota and Iowa and Missouri...now they set out to go across Kansas...There was only the enormous, empty prairie, with grasses blowing in waves of light and shadow across it, and the great blue sky above it, and birds flying up from it and singing with joy because the sun was rising. And on the whole enormous prairie there was no sign that any other human being had ever been there.

Laura Ingalls Wilder (1867-1957)
Little House on the Prairie

I believe that if one always looked at the skies, one would end up with wings.

Gustave Flaubert (1821-1880)
Pensées de Gustave Flaubert

Does the road wind up-hill all the way?
Yes, to the very end.
Will the day's journey take the whole long day?
From morn to night, my friend.

Christina Rossetti (1830-1894)
'Up-hill', *The Unseen World*

They went to sea in a sieve, they did;
In a sieve they went to sea;
In spite of all their friends could say.

Edward Lear (1812-1888)
The Jumblies

To travel hopefully is a better thing than to arrive, and true success is to labour.

Robert Louis Stevenson (1850-1894)
'El Dorado', *Virginibus Puerisque*

Listen, my children, and you shall hear
Of the midnight ride of Paul Revere,
On the eighteenth of April in Seventy-five.

Henry Wadsworth Longfellow (1807-1882)
'The Landlord's Tale: Paul Revere's Ride', *Tales of a Wayside Inn*

Of all noxious animals, too, the most noxious is a tourist. And of all tourists, the most vulgar, ill-bred, offensive and loathsome is the British tourist.

Francis Kilvert (1840-1879)
Diary, 5 April, 1870

Nowhere to go but out,
Nowhere to come but back.

Benjamin Franklin King (1857-1894)
'The Pessimist'

Give to me the life that I love,
Let the lave go by me,
Give the jolly heaven above
And the byway nigh me.
Bed in the bush with stars to see,
Bread I dip in the river –
There's the life for a man like me,
There's the life for ever.

Robert Louis Stevenson (1850-1894)
Songs of Travel 'The Vagabond'

The religious inebriation of big cities.—
Pantheism.
I am everyone; everyone is me.
Whirlwind.

Charles Baudelaire (1821–1867)
'My heart laid bare'

Long I roam'd the woods of the north—long I watch'd Niagara pouring;
I travel'd the prairies over, and slept on their breast—
I cross'd the Nevadas, I cross'd the plateaus;
I ascended the towering rocks along the Pacific, I sail'd out to sea;
I sail'd through the storm, I was refresh'd by the storm;
I watch'd with joy the threatening maws of the waves;

Walt Whitman (1819-1892)
'Rise, O Days'

I cannot rest from travel: I will drink
Life to the lees: all times I have enjoy'd
Greatly, have suffer'd greatly, both with those
That lov'd me, and alone; on shore, and when
Thro' scudding drifts the rainy Hyades
Vex'd the dim sea. I am become a name;
For always roaming with a hungry heart
Much have I seen and known: cities of men
And manners, climates, councils, governments,
Myself not least, but honor'd of them all; And
drunk delight of battle with my peers,
Far on the ringing plains of windy Troy.
I am a part of all that I have met;

Yet all experience is an arch wherethro'
Gleams that untravell'd world, whose margin fades
For ever and for ever when I move.

Alfred, Lord Tennyson (1809-1892)
'Ulysses'

Wealth I ask not, hope nor love,
Nor a friend to know me;
All I ask: the heaven above
And the road below me.

Robert Louis Stevenson (1850-1894)
'The Vagabond', *Songs of Travel*

On the hilltop above me sat the rising moon; pale yet as a cloud, but brightening momently; she looked over Hay, which, half lost in trees, sent up a blue smoke from its few chimneys; it was yet a mile distant, but in the absolute hush I could hear plainly its thin murmers of life. My ear, too, felt the flow of currents; in what dales and depths I could not tell: but there were many hills beyond Hay, and doubtless many becks threading their passes. That evening calm betrayed alike the tinkle of the nearest streams, the sough of the most remote.

A rude noise broke out on these fine ripplings and whisperings, at once so far away and so clear: a positive tramp, tramp, a metallic clatter, which effaced the soft wave-wanderings; as, in a picture, the solid mass of a crag, or the rough boles of a great oak, drawn in dark and strong in the foreground, efface the aerial distance of azure hill, sunny horizon, and blended clouds, where tint melts into tint.

The din was on the causeway: a horse was coming.

Charlotte Brontë (1816-1855)
Jane Eyre, ch. 12

My bonnie lass, what aileth thee,
On this bright summer day,
To travel sad and shoeless thus
Upon the stony way?

John Stuart Blackie (1809-1850)
'The Emigrant Lassie'

Now when thus mounting the hill Zarathustra thought on his way of his many lonely wanderings from his youth, and how many hills and mountain ridges and summits had been ascended by him.

'I am a wanderer and a mountain-climber,' he said unto his heart; 'I like not the plains, and it seemeth I cannot long sit still.'

'And whatever may become my fate and experience, a wandering and a mountain-climbing will be part of it. In the end one experienceth nothing but one's self.'

Friedrich Nietzsche (1844-1900)
Thus Spake Zarathustra

This fertile and sheltered tract of country, in which the fields are never brown and the springs never dry, is bounded on the south by the bold chalk ridge that embraces the prominences of Hambledon Hill, Bulbarrow, Nettlecombe-Tout, Dogbury, High Stoy, and Bubb Down. The traveller from the coast, who, after plodding northward for a score of miles over the calcareous downs and corn-lands, suddenly reaches the verge of one of these escarpments, is surprised and delighted to behold, extended like a map beneath him, a country differing absolutely from that which he has passed through. Behind him the hills are open, the sun blazes down upon the fields so large as to give an unenclosed character to the landscape, the lanes are white, the hedges low and plashed, the atmosphere colourless. Here, in the valley, the world seems to be constructed upon a smaller and more delicate scale…

Thomas Hardy (1840–1928)
Tess of the D'Urbervilles, ch. 2

All things journey: sun and moon,
Morning, noon, and afternoon,
Night and all her stars:
'Twixt the east and western bars
Round they journey,
Come and go.
We go with them!
For to roam and ever roam
Is the Zíncali's loved home.

George Eliot (1819–1880)
'The Song of the Zíncali', *Songs from the Spanish Gypsy ii*

Any landsman seeing the Milky Way would have nightmare for a week.

Charles Darwin (1809-1882)
Journal aboard the Beagle

It is a far, far better thing that I do, than I have ever done; it is a far, far better rest, that I go to, than I have ever known.

Charles Dickens (1812-1870)
A Tale of Two Cities, ch. 15

In God's wildness lies the hope of the world—the great fresh unblighted, unredeemed wilderness. The galling harness of civilization drops off, and the wounds heal ere we are aware.

John Muir (1838–1914)
Alaska Fragment

Every man paddle his own canoe

Captain Frederick Marryat (1792-1848)
Settlers in Canada, ch. 8

For the journey is done and the summit attained,
And the barriers fall,
Though a battle's to fight ere the guerdon be gained,
The reward of it all.

Robert Browning (1812-1889)
'Prospice'

There was no possibility of taking a walk that day. We had been wandering, indeed, in the leafless shrubbery an hour in the morning; but since dinner (Mrs Reed, when there was no company, dined early) the cold winter wind had brought with it clouds so sombre, and a rain so penetrating, that further outdoor exercise was now out of the question.

Charlotte Brontë (1816-1855)
Jane Eyre, ch. 1

A whaleship was my Yale College and my Harvard

Herman Melville (1819-1891)
Moby Dick, ch. 3

When the sun dawn'd,
O, gay and glad
We set the sail and plied the oar;
But when the night-wind blew like breath,
For joy of one day's voyage more,
We sang together on the wide sea,
Like men at peace on a peaceful shore;

Robert Browning (1812-1889)
'The Wanderers'

It was the Dover road that lay, on a Friday evening late in November, before the first of the persons with whom this history has business. The Dover road lay, as to him, beyond the Dover mail, as it lumbered up Shooter's Hill. He walked up-hill in the mire by the side of the mail, as the rest of the passengers did; not because they had the least relish for walking exercise, under the circumstances, but because the hill, and the harness, and the mud, and the mail, were all so heavy, that the horses had three times already come to a stop, besides once drawing the coach across the road, with the mutinous intent of taking it back to Blackheath. Reins and whip and coachman and guard, however, in combination, had read that article of war which forbad a purpose otherwise strongly in favour of the argument, that some brute animals are endued with Reason; and the team had capitulated and returned to their duty.

Charles Dickens (1812-1870)
A Tale of Two Cities, Book 1, ch. 2

Fatal Africa! One after another, travellers drop away. It is such a huge continent, and each of its secrets is environed by many difficulties – the torrid heat, the miasma exhaled from the soil, the noisome vapours enveloping every path, the giant cane-grass suffocating the wayfarer, the rabid fury of the native guarding every entry and exit, the unspeakable misery of the life within the wild continent, the utter absence of every comfort...

Henry Morton Stanley (1841-1904)
Autobiography

Let us arise and go like men,
And face with an undaunted tread
The long black passage up to bed.

Robert Louis Stevenson (1850-1894)
'North-West Passage. Good Night.',
A Child's Garden of Verse

Only by going alone in silence, without baggage, can one truly get into the heart of the wilderness. All other travel is mere dust and hotels and baggage and chatter.

John Muir (1838-1914)
Life and Letters of John Muir

Round the cape of a sudden came the sea,
And the sun look'd over the mountain's rim:
And straight was a path of gold for him,
And the need of a world of men for me

Robert Browning (1812-1889)
'Parting at Morning'

Railroads shall soon traverse all this country, and with a rattle and a glare the engine and train shall shoot like a meteor over the wide night-landscape, turning the moon paler; but, as yet, such things are non-existent in these parts, though not wholly unexpected. Preparations are afoot, measurements are made, ground is staked out. Bridges are begun, and their not yet united piers desolately look at one another over roads and streams, like brick and mortar couples with an obstacle to their union; fragments of embankments are thrown up, and left as precipices with torrents of rusty carts and barrows tumbling over them; tripods of tall poles appear on hilltops, where there are rumours of tunnels; everything looks chaotic, and abandoned in full hopelessness. Along the freezing roads, and through the night, the post-chaise makes its way without a railroad on its mind.

Charles Dickens (1812-1870)
Bleak House, ch. 55

Better sleep with a sober cannibal than a drunken Christian

Herman Melville (1819-1891)
Moby Dick, ch. 3

He has gone to Hell or Kentucky

Saying, Wild West

O, to be in England
Now that April's there,
And whoever wakes in England
Sees, some morning, unaware,

That the lowest boughs and the brushwood sheaf
Round the elm-tree bole are in tiny leaf,
While the chaffinch sings on the orchard bough
In England—now!

Robert Browning (1812-1889)
'Home-thoughts from Abroad'

The discovery of America, the rounding of the Cape, opened up fresh ground for the rising bourgeoisie. The East-Indian and Chinese markets, the colonization of America, trade with the colonies, the increase in the means of exchange and in commodities generally, gave to commerce, to navigation, to industry, an impulse never before known, and thereby, to the revolutionary element in the tottering feudal society, a rapid development.

Marx (1818-1883) and **Engels** (1820-1895)
The Communist Manifesto

The road to the City of Emeralds is paved with yellow brick.

L Frank Baum (1856-1919)
The Wonderful Wizard of Oz

Far travel, very far travel, or travail, comes near to the worth of staying at home.

Henry David Thoreau (1817-1862)
The Writings of Henry David Thoreau

I never travel without my diary. One should always have something sensational to read in the train.

Oscar Wilde (1854-1900)
The Importance of Being Earnest, Act 3

And now my written story ends. I look back, once more – for the last time—before I close these leaves.

I see myself, with Agnes at my side, journeying along the road of life. I see our children and our friends around us; and I hear the roar of many voices, not indifferent to me as I travel on.

Charles Dickens (1812-1870)
David Copperfield, ch. 64

When at last I got well enough to travel, I set my face toward the east, and journeyed on foot through the northern coal regions of Pennsylvania by slow stages, caring little whither I went, and earning just enough by peddling flat-irons to pay my way. It was spring when I started; the autumn tints were on the leaves when I brought up in New York at last, as nearly restored as youth and the long tramp had power to do. But the restless energy that had made of me a successful salesman was gone. I thought only, if I thought at all, of finding some quiet place where I could sit and see the world go by that concerned me no longer.

Jacob A Riis (1849-1914)
The Making of an American, ch. 5

A man may travel fast enough and earn his living on the road.

Henry David Thoreau (1817-1862)
The Writings of Henry David Thoreau

Bachelors alone can travel freely, and without any twinges of their consciences touching desertion of the fire-side.

Herman Melville (1819-1891)
The Paradise of Bachelors and the Tartarus of Maids

When it was first proposed that I should go abroad, or how it came to be agreed among us that I was to seek the restoration of my peace in change and travel, I do not, even now, distinctly know.

Charles Dickens (1812-1870)
David Copperfield, ch. 54

Though we travel the world over to find the beautiful, we must carry it with us, or we find it not

Ralph Waldo Emerson (1803-1882)
'Art', *Essays*

Let us take to us, now that the white skies thrill with a moon unarisen,
Swift horses of fear or of love, take flight and depart and not die.
They are swifter than dreams, they are stronger than death; there is none that hath ridden,
None that shall ride in the dim strange ways of his life as we ride:
By the meadows of memory, the highlands of hope, and the shore that is hidden,

Where life breaks loud and unseen, a sonorous invisible tide;
By the sands where sorrow has trodden, the salt pools bitter and sterile,
By the thundering reef and the low sea wall and the channel of years,
Our wild steeds press on the night, strain hard through pleasure and peril,
Labour and listen and pant not or pause for the peril that nears

Algernon Charles Swinburne (1837-1909)
'Hesperia'

Duchess of Berwick: Dear girl! She is so fond of photographs of Switzerland. Such a pure taste, I think.

Oscar Wilde (1854-1900)
Lady Windermere's Fan

Roads are made for horses and men of business. I do not travel in them much.

Henry David Thoreau (1817-1862)
'Walking', *The Writings of Henry David Thoreau*

The uses of travel are occasional, and short; but the best fruit it finds, when it finds it, is conversation; and this is a main function of life.

Ralph Waldo Emerson (1803-1882)
'Considerations by the Way', *The Conduct of Life*

For the profit of travel: in the first place, you get rid of a few prejudices... The prejudiced against colour finds several hundred millions of people of all shades of colour, and all degrees of intellect, rank, and social worth, generals, judges, priests, and kings, and learns to give up his foolish prejudice.

Herman Melville (1819-1891)
Traveling

Spirit of place! It is for this we travel, to surprise its subtlety; and where it is a strong and dominant angel, that place, seen once, abides entire in the memory with all its own accidents, its habits, its breath, its name.

Alice Meynell (1847-1922),
'The Spirit of Place', *Essays*

Henceforth I whimper no more, postpone no more, need nothing,
Done with indoor complaints, libraries, querulous criticisms,
Strong and content I travel the open road.

Walt Whitman (1819-1892)
'Song of the Open Road'

Modesty and taste are questions of latitude and education; the more people know,—the more their ideas are expanded by travel, experience, and observation,—the less easily they are shocked. The narrowness and bigotry of women are the result of their circumscribed sphere of thought and action.

Elizabeth Cady Stanton (1815-1902)
Eighty Years and More, ch. 6

I have found out that there ain't no surer way to find out whether you like people or hate them than to travel with them.

Mark Twain (1835-1910),
Tom Sawyer Abroad, ch. 11

People imagine that a long voyage must be restful and peaceful, but really it may become more strenuous than ordinary life. For example, we have a French lesson morning and evening under the tuition of a French acrobat from the second class. There is an interminable list of competitions of various kinds for the youngsters. There is a daily swim for every one in the big salt-water bath. There are concerts and dances every evening. I have been asked to lecture upon psychic subjects on Sunday. Add to this the constant companionship, the writing of letters, and the use of a good library, and no one should find the time hang heavy...Tomorrow we shall lie in Table Bay, ending one chapter of our lives and beginning another.

Arthur Conan Doyle (1859-1930)
Our African Winter

To get away from one's working environment is, in a sense, to get away from one's self; and this is often the chief advantage of travel and change.

Charles Horton Cooley (1864-1929),
Human Nature and the Social Order, ch. 6

What is there in Rome for me to see that others have not seen before me? What is there for me to touch that others have not touched? What is there for me to feel, to learn, to hear, to know, that shall thrill me before it pass to others? What can I discover?—Nothing. Nothing whatsoever. One charm of travel dies here.

Mark Twain (1835-1910)
The Innocents Abroad, ch. 26

One approaches the journey's end. But the end is a goal, not a catastrophe.

George Sand (1804-1876)
Diary entry, September, 1868

Egypt is not the country to go for the recreation of travel. It is too suggestive and too confounding...

Harriet Martineau (1802-1876)
Eastern Life, Present and Past

After having been twice driven back by heavy southwestern gales, Her Majesty's ship Beagle, a ten-gun brig, under the command of Captain Fitz Roy, R. N., sailed from Devonport on the 27th of December, 1831. The object of the expedition was to complete the survey of Patagonia and Tierra del Fuego, commenced under Captain King in 1826 to 1830—to survey the shores of Chile, Peru, and of some islands in the Pacific—and to carry a chain of chronometrical measurements round the World.

Charles Darwin (1809-1882)
The Voyage of the Beagle, ch 1

For like a mole I journey in the dark,
A-travelling along the underground

John Davidson (1857-1909)
'Thirty Bob a Week'

For when the gallows is high
Your journey is shorter to heaven.

Unknown
'The Night before Larry Was Stretched'

The journey I find briefly set down in my pocket-book as thus: - Cairo Gardens – Mosquitoes – Women dressed in blue – Children dressed in nothing – Old Cairo – Nile, dirty water, ferry-boat – Town – Palm-trees, town – Rice fields – Maize fields – Fellows on Dromedaries – Donkey down – Over his head – Pick up pieces – More palm-trees – More rice fields – Watercourses – Howling Arabs – Donkey tumbles down again – Inundations – Herons or cranes – Broken bridges – Sand – Pyramids. If a man cannot make a landscape out of that he had no imagination...You may shut your eyes and imagine yourself there. It is the pleasantest way, entre nous.

W M Thackeray (1811-1863)
Punch in the East

Up, lad: when the journey's over
There'll be time enough to sleep.

A E Housman (1859-1936)
'Reveille', *A Shropshire Lad*

I am reminded by my journey how exceedingly new this country still is. You have only to travel for a few days into the interior and back parts even of many of the old States, to come to that very America which the Northmen, and Cabot, and Gosnold, and Smith, and Raleigh visited.

Henry David Thoreau (1817-1862)
'Ktaadn', *The Writings of Henry David Thoreau*

This is the land that flowed with milk and honey. As a matter of fact it flows now chiefly with stones.

Lilian Leland (b.1857)
On Palestine, Travelling Alone, A Woman's Journal round the World 1890

On desperate seas long wont to roam,
Thy hyacinth hair, thy classic face,
Thy Naiad airs have brought me home
To the glory that was Greece,
And the grandeur that was Rome.

Edgar Allen Poe (1809-1849)
'To Helen'

This country strikes a person at first glance as being immensely rich in the precious metals. But 'All that glitters is not gold' I found a very true proverb. In my prospecting tour over the mountains, I saw quantities of yellow metal which I believed to be gold. I filled my pockets with the precious stuff, as there was so much of it. I filled a satchel with it, and had a very good mind to fill my hat also. I carried my treasure to the hotel, and up to my room, and, choosing a small piece, I took it down, and carelessly asked a rough-looking fellow what he thought of it. Imagine my surprise and disappointment when he pronounced it a 'pretty nice specimen of pyrites of iron.' All my castles in the air had vanished; the great good I was about to do mankind had to be postponed; and my fine house, with all its magnificent appurtenances, I was obliged to defer to some other day.'

Henry Morton Stanley (1841-1904)
My Early Travels and Adventures in America and Asia

England will never be civilized till she has added Utopia to her dominions.

Oscar Wilde (1854-1900)
The Critic as Artist

In a flash she remembered the man who had been run down by the train the day she first met Vronsky, and knew what she had to do. Quickly and lightly she descended the steps that led from the water-tank to the rails, and stopped close to the passing train. She looked at the lower part of the trucks, at the bolts and chains and the tall iron wheels of the first truck slowly moving up, and tried to measure the point midway between the front and back wheels, and the exact moment when it would be opposite her.

'There,' she said to herself, looking in the shadow of the truck at the mixture of sand and coal dust which covered the sleepers. 'There, in the very middle, and I shall punish him and escape from them all and from myself.'

Leo Tolstoy (1828-1910)
Anna Karenina, part 7, ch. 31

All scenery in California requires distance to give it its highest charm

Mark Twain (1835–1910)
Roughing It

They traveled 2nd class in the train and Ethel was longing to go first but thought perhaps least said soonest mended. Mr Salteena got very excited in the train about his visit. Ethel was calm but she felt excited inside. Bernard has a big house said Mr S. gazing at Ethel he is inclined to be rich.

Oh indeed said Ethel looking at some cows flashing past the window. Mr S. felt rather disheartened so he read the paper till the train stopped and the porters shouted Rickamere station. We had better collect our traps said Mr Salteena and just then a very exalted footman in a cocked hat and olive green uniform put his head in the window. Are you for Rickamere Hall he said in very impressive tones.

Well yes I am said Mr Salteena and so is this lady. Very good sir said the noble footman if you alight I will see to your luggage there is a conveyance awaiting you.

Oh thankyou thankyou said Mr S. and he and Ethel stepped along the platform. Outside they found a lovely carriage lined with olive green cushions to match the footman and the horses had green bridles and bows on their manes and tails. They got gingerly in. Will he bring our luggage asked Ethel nervously.

Daisy Ashford (1881-1972)
The Young Visiters, ch. 2

Still, the last sad memory hovers round, and sometimes drifts across like floating mist, cutting off sunshine and chilling the remembrance of happier times. There have been joys too great to be described in words, and there have been griefs upon which I have not dared to dwell; and with these in mind I say: Climb if you will, but remember that courage and strength are nought without prudence, and that a momentary negligence may destroy the happiness of a lifetime. Do nothing in haste; look well to each step; and from the beginning think what may be the end.

Edward Whymper (1840-1911)
Scrambles amongst the Alps.

St Joseph in 1859 had the bustling appearance of a great fair, with excited travelers preparing to make the plains journey in prairie schooners, 'rickety old farm wagons,' and even small two-wheeled push carts. Many bore such mottoes as—'Faint Heart Never Won Fair Lady,' 'I Dare,' 'For Pike's Peak Ho.' Before long many were to return, disappointed in their search for gold, hungry, ragged, and dispirited, their brave wagon boasts changed to 'Prodigal Son,' 'Pike's Hell,' 'A Fool Is Born.'

Unknown
Missouri: A Guide to the 'Show Me' State, 1941

Casey Jones, mounted to the cabin,
Casey Jones, throttle in his hand,
Casey Jones mounted to the cabin,
Took his farewell journey to the Promised Land.

Unknown
'Casey Jones'

Many an evening hour the five sisters took one another by the arm and rose up in a row over the water. They had splendid voices, more charming than any mortal could have; and when a storm was approaching, so that they could apprehend that ships would go down, they swam on before the ships and sang lovely songs, which told how beautiful it was at the bottom of the sea, and exhorted the sailors not to be afraid to come down. But these could not understand the words, and thought it was the storm sighing; and they did not see the splendours below, for if the ships sank they were drowned, and came as corpses to the Sea-king's palace.

Hans Christian Anderson (1805-1875)
The Little Sea Maid

This century fulfils the office of road-labourer for the society of the future. We make the road, others will make the journey.

Victor Hugo (1802-1885)
'Thoughts', *Victor Hugo's Intellectual Autobiograhy*

Go out of the house to see the moon, and 'tis mere tinsel; it will not please as when its light shines upon your necessary journey. The beauty that shimmers in the yellow afternoons of October, who could ever clutch it? Go forth to find it, and it is gone: 'tis only a mirage as you look from the windows of diligence.

Ralph Waldo Emerson (1803-1882)
'Nature', ch. 3

Captain FitzRoy being anxious that some bearings should be taken on the outer coast of Chile, it was planned that Mr King and myself should ride to Castro, and thence across the island to the Capella de Cucao, situated on the west coast. Having hired horses and a guide, we set out on the morning of the 22nd. We had not proceeded far, before we were joined by a woman and two boys, who were bent on the same journey. Every one on this road acts on a 'hail fellow well met' fashion; and one may here enjoy the privilege, so rare in South America, of travelling without firearms

Charles Darwin (1809-1882)
The Voyage of the Beagle

Thy pardon, Father, I beseech,
In this my prayer if I offend;
One something sees beyond his reach
From childhood to his journey's end.
My wife, our little boy Aignan,
Have travelled even to Narbonne;
My grandchild has seen Perpignan;
And I—have not seen Carcassonne.

Gustave Nadaud (1820-1893)
'Carcassone'

It was wonderful to find America, but it would have been more wonderful to miss it

Mark Twain (1835-1910)
Pudd'nhead Wilson's Calendar

Progress is the life-style of man. The general life of the human race is called Progress, and so is its collective march. Progress advances, it makes the great human and earthly journey towards what is heavenly and divine; it has its pauses, when it rallies the stragglers, its stopping places when it meditates, contemplating some new and splendid promised land that has suddenly appeared on its horizon. It has its nights of slumber; and it is one of the poignant anxieties of the thinker to see the human spirit lost in shadow, and to grope in the darkness without being able to awake sleeping progress.

Victor Hugo (1802-1885)
Les Misérables, part 5, Book 1, ch. 20

My voyages (in paper boats) among savages often yield me matter for reflection at home

Charles Dickens (1812-1870)
The Uncommercial Traveller

Absolute continuity of motion is not comprehensible to the human mind. Laws of motion of any kind only become comprehensible to man when he examines arbitrarily selected elements of that motion; but at the same time, a large proportion of human error comes from the arbitrary division of continuous motion into discontinuous elements. There is a well-known, so-called, sophism of the ancients consisting in this, that Achilles could never catch up with a tortoise he was following in spite of the fact that he travelled ten times as fast as the tortoise. By the time Achilles has covered the distance that separated him from the tortoise, the tortoise has covered one-tenth of that distance ahead of him; when Achilles has covered that tenth, the tortoise has covered another one-hundredth and so on for ever. This problem seemed to the ancients insoluble. The absurd answer (that Achilles could never overtake the tortoise) resulted from this: that motion was arbitrarily divided into discontinuous elements, whereas the motion both of Achilles and of the tortoise was continuous.

Leo Tolstoy (1828-1910)
War and Peace Book XI, ch. 1

What's the good of home if you are never in it?

George and Weedon Grossmith (1847-1912/ 1854-1919) *The Diary of A Nobody*, ch.1

Dark spruce forest frowned on either side of the frozen waterway. The trees had been stripped by a recent wind of their white covering of frost, and they seemed to lean toward each other, black and ominous, in the fading light. A vast silence reigned over the land. The land itself was a desolation, lifeless, without movement, so lone and cold that the spirit of it was not even that of sadness. There was a hint in it of laughter, but of a laughter more terrible than any sadness – a laughter that was mirthless as the smile of the Sphinx, a laughter cold as the frost and partaking of the grimness of infallibility. It was the masterful and incommunicable wisdom of eternity laughing at the futility of life and the effort of life. It was the Wild, the savage, frozen-hearted North-land Wild.

Jack London (1876-1916)
White Fang

It is good to collect things; it is better to take walks.

Anatole France (1844-1924)

O ye tak' the high road and I'll tak' the low road,
And I'll be in Scotland afore ye

The Bonnie Banks of Loch Lomond

We had to walk home in the pouring rain, nearly two miles, and when I got in I put down the conversation I had with the cabman, word for word, as I intend writing to the *Telegraph* for the purpose of proposing that cabs should be driven only by men under Government control, to prevent civilians being subjected to the disgraceful insults and injury that I had to endure.

George and Weedon Grossmith (1847-1912/1854-1919) *The Diary of A Nobody,* ch.18

Ah! What is man? Wherefore does he why? Whence did he whence? Whither is he whithering?

Dan Leno (1860-1904)
Dan Leno Hys Booke

Travel is fatal to prejudice, bigotry, and narrow-mindedness, and many of our people need it sorely on these accounts.

Mark Twain (1835-1910)
The Innocents Abroad

May the road rise with you, and the wind be ever at your back

Irish toast

I collided with some 'trippers'
In my swift De Dion Bouton;
Squased them out as flat as kippers,
Left them *aussi mort que mouton.*
What a nuisance 'trippers' are!
Now I must repaint the car.

Harry Graham (1874-1936)
'Inconvenience', *Ruthless Rhymes for Heartless Homes*

Going up that river was like travelling back to the earliest beginnings of the world, when vegetations rioted on the earth and the big trees were kings. An empty stream, a great silence, an impenetrable forest. The air was warm, thick, heavy, sluggish. There was no joy in the brilliance of sunshine. The long stretches of the waterway ran on, deserted, into the gloom of overshadowed distances. On silvery sandbanks hippos and alligators sunned themselves side by side. The broadening waters flowed through a mob of wooded islands; you lost your way on that river as you would in a desert, and butted all day long against shoals, trying to find the channel, till you thought yourself bewitched and cut off for ever from everything you had known once – somewhere – far away – in another existence perhaps. There were moments when one's past came back to one, as it will sometimes when you have not a moment to spare to yourself; but it came in the shape of an unrestful and noisy dream, remembered with wonder amongst the overwhelming realities of this strange world of plants, and water, and silence. And this stillness of life did not in the least resemble a peace. It was the stillness of an implacable force brooding over an inscrutable intention. It looked at you with a vengeful aspect.

Joseph Conrad (1857-1924)
Heart of Darkness

My bonnie lies over the ocean
My bonnie lies over the sea
My bonnie lies over the ocean
Oh bring back my bonnie to me.

Traditional song

I had written to Aunt Maud,
Who was on a trip abroad,
When I heard she'd died of cramp.
Just too late to save the stamp.

Harry Graham (1874–1936)
'Waste', *Ruthless Rhymes for Heartless Homes*

A little further on was the summit whence Christminster, or what he had taken for that city, had seemed to be visible. A milestone, now as always, stood at the roadside hard by. Jude drew near it, and felt rather than read the mileage to the city. He remembered that once on his way home he had proudly cut with his keen new chisel an inscription on the back of the milestone, embodying his aspirations. It had been done in the first week of his apprenticeship, before he had been diverted from his purposes by an unsuitable woman. He wondered if the inscription were legible still, and going to the back of the milestone brushed away the nettles. By the light of a match he could still discern what he had cut so enthusiastically so long ago:

THITHER →

J.F.

Thomas Hardy (1840-1928)
Jude the Obscure, Part 1, ch. 11

My father and mother in 1817 were forty-nine days on the road with their emigrant wagons [from Vermont] to Ohio. More than two days for each hour that I spent in the same journey.

Rutherford Birchard Hayes (1822-1893)
US President, diary entry, December 29, 1891

Come, my friends,
'Tis not too late to seek a newer world.
Push off, and sitting well in order smite
The sounding furrows; for my purpose holds
To sail beyond the sunset, and the baths
Of all the western stars, until I die.

Alfred, Lord Tennyson (1809-1892)
'Ulysses'

April 27th.—I set out on a journey to Coquimbo, and thence through Guasco to Copiapó, where Captain FitzRoy kindly offered to pick me up in the *Beagle*. The distance in a straight line along the shore northward is only 420 miles; but my mode of travelling made it a very long journey. I bought four horses and two mules, the latter carrying the luggage on alternate days. The six animals together only cost the value of twenty-five pounds sterling, and at Copiapó I sold them again for twenty-three. We travelled in the same independent manner as before, cooking our own meals, and sleeping in the open air. As we rode towards the Viño del Mar, I took a farewell view of Valparaiso, and admired its picturesque appearance.

Charles Darwin (1809-1882)
The Voyage of the Beagle, ch. XVI

The man should have youth and strength who seeks adventure in the wide, waste spaces of the earth, in the marshes, and among the vast mountain masses, in the northern forests, amid the steaming jungles of the tropics, or on the deserts of sand or of snow.

Theodore Roosevelt (1858-1919)
A Book-Lover's Holidays in the Open

That was a wonderful trunk. So soon as any one pressed the lock the trunk could fly. He pressed it, and whirr! away flew the trunk with him through the chimney and over the clouds, farther and farther away. But as often as the bottom of the trunk cracked a little he was in great fear lest it might go to pieces, and then he would have flung a fine somersault! In that way he came to the land of the Turks. He hid the trunk in a wood under some dry leaves, and then went into the town. He could do that very well, for among the Turks all the people went about dressed like himself in dressing-gown and slippers.

Hans Christian Anderson (1805-1875)
The Flying Trunk

Mountains are the beginning and end of all natural scenery

John Ruskin (1819-1900)
Modern Painters

To cross the Pacific Ocean, even under the most favourable circumstances, brings you for many days close to nature, and you realise the vastness of the sea. Slowly but surely the mark of my little ship's course on the track-chart reached out on the ocean and across it, while at her utmost speed she marked with her keel still slowly the sea that carried her.

Joshua Slocum (1844-1909)
Sailing Alone Around The World

Dr Livingstone, I presume?

Henry Morton Stanley (1841-1904)
How I found Livingstone, ch. 11

A man travels the world in search of what he needs and returns home to find it.

George Moore (1852-1933)
The Brook Kerith

Out where the handclap's a little stronger,
Out where the smile dwells a little longer,
That's where the West begins.

Arthur Chapman (1873-1935)
'Out Where the West Begins'

Upon reaching the bay the second time I had circumnavigated the wildest part of desolate Tierra del Fuego. But the *Spray* had not yet arrived at St Nicholas, and by the merest accident her bones were saved from resting there when she did arrive. The parting of a staysailsheet in a williwaw, when the sea was turbulent and she was plunging into the storm, brought me forward to see instantly a dark cliff ahead and breakers so close under the bows that I felt surely lost, and in my thoughts cried, 'Is the hand of fate against me, after all, leading me in the end to this dark spot?'

Joshua Slocum (1844-1909)
Sailing Alone Around The World

Swing low, sweet chariot—
Comin' for to carry me home;
I looked over Jordan and what did I see?
A band of angels comin' after me—
Comin' for to carry me home.

Negro Spiritual

One flew east and one flew west
And one flew over the cuckoo's nest

Traditional American rhyme

Nothing is more striking to an American than the frequency of English holidays and the large way in which occasions for a 'little change' are made use of. All this speaks to Americans of three things which they are accustomed to see allotted in scantier measure. The English have more time than we, they have more money, and they have a much higher relish for active leisure. Leisure, fortune, and the love of sport - these things are implied in English society at every turn.

Henry James (1843-1916)
Portraits of Places, ch. 9

Walk! Not bloody likely. I am going in a taxi.

George Bernard Shaw (1856-1950)
Pygmalion, Act 3

We travel not for travelling alone,
By a greater heat our fiery hearts are fanned,
For lust of knowing what should not be known
We take the Golden Road to Samarkand.

James Elroy Flecker (1884-1915)
'The Golden Road to Samarkand'

He who would travel happily must travel light.

Antoine de Saint-Exupéry (1900-1944)

When you travel, remember that a foreign country is not designed to make you comfortable. It is designed to make its own people comfortable.

Clifton Fadiman (b.1904-)

Discovery is adventure. There is an eagerness, touched at times with tenseness, as man moves ahead into the unknown. Walking the wilderness is indeed like living. The horizon drops away, bringing new sights, sounds, and smells from the earth. When one moves through the forests, his sense of discovery is quickened. Man is back in the environment from which he emerged to build factories, churches, and schools. He is primitive again, matching his wits against the earth and sky. He is free of the restraints of society and free of its safeguards too.

William O Douglas (1898-1980)
Of Men and Mountains

To get through their days, nervous natures such as mine have various 'speeds' as do automobiles. There are uphill and difficult days which take an eternity to climb, and downhill days which can be quickly descended.

Marcel Proust (1871-1922)
Remembrance of Things Past, vol I, Swann's Way

The two cities at the Atlantic entrance of the Panama Canal, Cristobal and Colon, are the true names of Columbus. He never signed his name any other way than 'Cristobal Colon'.

Robert L Ripley (1890-1949)
Believe It or Not!

The books one reads in childhood, and perhaps most of all the bad and good bad books, create in one's mind a sort of false map of the world, a series of fabulous countries into which one can retreat at odd moments throughout the rest of life, and which in some cases can survive a visit to the real countries which they are supposed to represent.

George Orwell (1903-1950)
'Riding Down from Bangor'

When I went to Venice – my dream became my address

Marcel Proust (1871-1922)
Letter to Madame Strauss, c. May 1906

Lucy said that this was most kind, and at once opened the Baedeker, to see where Santa Croce was.

'Tut, tut! Miss Lucy! I hope we shall soon emancipate you from Baedeker. He does but touch the surface of things. As to the true Italy – he does not even dream of it. The true Italy is only to be found by patient observation.'

E M Forster (1879-1970)
A Room with a View, ch. 2

His attitude to foreign travel, at least since he had had the means at his disposal to enjoy its advantages as often as he pleased, had always been that it was nothing more than a necessary health precaution, to be taken from time to time however disinclined to it one might be.

Thomas Mann (1875-1955)
Death In Venice, ch. 1

To do nothing that can either annoy or offend the sensibilities of others, sums up the principal rules for conduct under all circumstances—whether staying at home or traveling. But in order to do nothing that can annoy or give offense, it is necessary for us to consider the point of view of those with whom we come in contact; and in traveling abroad it is necessary to know something of foreign customs which affect the foreign point of view, if we would be thought a cultivated and charming people instead of an uncivilized and objectionable one.

Emily Post (1873-1960)
'Traveling at Home and Abroad', *Etiquette*

If you and I were one, my dear,
  A model life we'd lead.
We'd travel on, from year to year
  At no increase of speed,
Ah, clear to me the vision of
  The things that we should do!
And so I think it best my love,
  To string along as two

Dorothy Parker (1893-1967)
'Day Dreams'

'My dear, I know I have inconvenienced you terribly by making you take your holiday now, and I know you did not really want to come to Yugoslavia at all. But when you get there you will see why it was so important that we should make this journey, and that we should make it now, at Easter. It will all be quite clear, once we are in Yugoslavia.'

There was, however, no reply. My husband had gone to sleep.

Rebecca West (1892-1983)
Prologue, *Black Lamb and Grey Falcon*

The past is a foreign country: they do things differently there.

L P Hartley (1895-1972)
The Go-Between

The Isle of Man, like Shakespeare, has something memorable for everyone. It is a place of strong contrasts and great variety. Yet in southern England it is hardly known at all.

Sir John Betjeman (1906-1984)
The Isle of Man, *Portraits of Islands*

Just thirty years ago two Norwegians rowed – actually rowed across the Atlantic from New York. They made no great fuss about it. They were in New York, the weather was fine so they reckoned they would row home and see how the old folks were getting on. Of course one ought to have a good, reliable rowing-boat, not a second-hand craft, so, like most wise cockleshell cruisers, they built her themselves, of well and truly seasoned cedar-wood. Eighteen feet long was she, clinker built, with a 5ft beam and a depth inside of 35 inches. Fox was her name. She dropped down the river from New York, on the outgoing tide, at five o'clock on the afternoon of June 6, 1896.

For more than a month the life of the rowers was relatively uneventful. The sun shone. The hills of swell went rolling majestically by. The oars were steadily plied, shift after shift. One ate. One sang. One slept.

Then things began to happen and their trip for the rest of the way was a nightmare. God was good to them, however, and eventually they made the port of Havre where they landed sixty-two days after leaving New York. By examing their log book and talking with them, Dr Chancellor, the openly sceptical American consul at that port, ascertained that this astounding feat had indeed been accomplished.

Robert L Ripley (1890–1949)
Believe It Or Not!

The true traveller is he who goes on foot, and even then, he sits down a lot of the time.

Colette (1873-1954)
Paris From My Window

Farewell my friends. I go to glory.

Isadora Duncan (1878-1927)
Last words

When I prepare for a journey I prepare as though for death. Should I never return, all is in order.

Katherine Mansfield (1888-1923)
Journal, 29 January 1922

A good traveller is one who does not know where he is going to, and a perfect traveller does not know where he came from.

Lin Yutang (1895-1976)
The Importance of Living

Theoretically, we know that the world turns, but in fact we do not notice it, the earth on which we walk does not seem to move and we live on in peace. This is how it is concerning Time in our lives. And to render its passing perceptible, novelists must...have their readers cross ten, twenty, thirty years in two minutes.

Marcel Proust (1871-1922)
Remembrance of Things Past, vol II

...get the greatest joy of travel even without going to the mountains, by staying at home and watching and going about the field to watch a sailing cloud, or a dog or a hedge, or a lonely tree.

Lin Yutang (1895-1976)
The Importance of Living

Venice is real great, but not cheap, no work here. Besides it's not exactly for me. There is something unreal about the place. It lacks depth, nuance and horror.

William S Burroughs (1914-1997)
From a letter to Bill Gilmore, July 26 1956

Last night I dreamt I went to Manderley again.

Daphne du Maurier (1907-1989)
Rebecca

Abroad is unutterably bloody, and foreigners are fiends

Nancy Mitford (1904-1973)
The Pursuit of Love

Surely it is worthwhile to pursue one of the last great adventures which the surface of the earth has to offer.

Hugh Ruttledge (1884-1961)
Everest 1933

Because it's there!

George Mallory (1886-1924)
on asked why he was climbing Everest

It looks like a picnic in Connemara surprised by a snowstorm

George Bernard Shaw (1856-1950)
On seeing a picture of Mallory's first Everest expedition

It has been well said that the first three rules of Himalayan mountaineering are: 'Reconnoitre, reconnoitre, and again reconnoitre.'

Hugh Ruttledge (1884-1961)
Everest 1933

To know a foreign country at all, you must not only have lived in it and in your own, but also lived in at least one other.

W Somerset Maugham (1874-1965)

Addresses are given to us to conceal our whereabouts.

Saki (1870-1916)

A long journey, even with the most lofty purpose, may be a dull thing to read of if it is made at leisure; but a hundred yards may be a breathless business if only a few seconds are granted to complete it.

John Buchan (1875-1940)
Preface, *A Book of Escapes and Hurried Journeys*

I am afraid I cannot convey the peculiar sensations of time travelling. They are excessively unpleasant. There is a feeling exactly like that one has upon a switchback – of a helpless, headlong motion!

H G Wells (1866-1946)
The Time Machine

When you come to a fork in the road, take it.

Yogi Berra (b.1925)

Men travel faster now, but I do not know if they go to better things.

Willa Cather (1873-1947)
Death Comes for the Archbishop

On passing our winter quarters at Cape Royds we all turned out to give three cheers, and to take a last look at the place where, in spite of discomforts and hardships, we had spent so many happy days. We watched the little hut, which had been our home for a year that must always live in our memories, fade away in the distance with feelings almost of sadness, and there were few men aboard who did not cherish a hope that some day they might again live strenuous days under the shadow of mighty Erebus.

Sir Ernest Shackleton (1874-1922)
The Heart of the Antartic

The poetry of motion! The real way to travel! The only way to travel! Here today – in next week tomorrow! Villages skipped, towns and cities jumped – always somebody else's horizon!

Kenneth Grahame (1859-1952)
The Wind in the Willows

This was the end. He slept through the night before last, hoping not to wake; but he woke in the morning – yesterday. It was blowing a blizzard. He said, 'I'm just going outside and may be some time.' He went out into the blizzard and we have not seen him since...we knew that poor Oates was walking to his death but though we tried to dissuade him, we knew it was the act of a brave man and an English gentleman. We all hope to meet the end with a similar spirit, and assuredly the end is not far off.

Captain R F Scott (1868-1912)
Scott's Last Expedition

They say travel broaden the minds; but you must have the mind.

G K Chesterton (1874-1936)
The Shadow of the Shark

Polar exploration is at once the cleanest and most isolated way of having a bad time which has been devised

Apsley Cherry-Garrard (1886-1959)
The Worst Journey in the World

We all have our own white south

Sir Ernest Shackleton (1874-1922)
The Heart of the Antartic

An adventure is only an inconvenience rightly considered. An inconvenience is only an adventure wrongly considered.

G K Chesterton (1874-1936)
All Things Considered

Every day we have been ready to start for our depot eleven miles away but outside the door of the tent it remains a scene of whirling drift. I do not think we can hope for any better things now. We shall stick it out to the end, but we are getting weaker, of course, and the end cannot be far.

It seems a pity but I do not think I can write more.

R Scott

For God's sake, look after our people.

Captain R F Scott (1868-1912)
Scott's Last Expedition

He was calm; however, he had to be supported during the journey through the long corridors, since he planted his feet unsteadily, like a child who has just learned to walk, or as if he were about to fall through like a man who has dreamt that he is walking on water only to have a sudden doubt: but is this possible?

Vladimir Nabokov (1899-1977)
Invitation to a Beheading, ch. 1

Such extremity of suffering cannot be measured. Madness or death may give relief. But this I know: we on this journey were already beginning to think of death as a friend.

Apsley Cherry-Garrard (1886-1959)
The Worst Journey in the World

Now it is autumn and the falling fruit
and the long journey towards oblivion.
The apples falling like great drops of dew
to bruise themselves an exit from themselves.

D H Lawrence (1885-1930)
'The Ship of Death'

One sees great things from the valley; only small things from the peak.

G K Chesterton (1874-1936)
The Innocence of Father Brown

And I tell you, if you have the desire for knowledge and the power to give it physical expression, go out and explore. If you are a brave man, you will do nothing: if you are fearful you may do much, for none but cowards have need to prove their bravery. Some will tell you that you are mad, and nearly all will say 'what is the use?'. For we are a nation of shopkeepers and no shopkeeper will look at research which does not promise him a financial return within a year. And so you will sledge nearly alone, but those with whom you sledge will not be shopkeepers; that is worth a good deal. If you march your Winter Journeys you will have your reward, so long as all you want is a penguin's egg.

Apsley Cherry-Garrard (1886-1959)
The Worst Journey in the World

We shall not cease from exploration
And the end of all our exploring
Will be to arrive where we started
And know the place for the first time.

T S Eliot (1888-1965)
'Little Gidding', *The Four Quartets*

[The ship] was an inhabitant of a great world, which has so few inhabitants, travelling all day across an empty universe, with veils drawn before her and behind. She was more lonely than a caravan crossing the desert; she was infinitely more mysterious, moving by her own power and sustained by her own resources. The sea might give her death or some unexampled joy, and none would know of it.

Virginia Woolf (1882-1941)
The Voyage Out

We must travel in the direction of our fear.

John Berryman (1914-1972)
'A Point of Age'

A merry road, a mazy road, and such as we did tread
The night we went to Birmingham by way of Beachy Head.

G K Chesterton (1874-1936)
The Rolling English Road

Take me back to dear old Blighty

A J Mills, Fred Godfrey & Bennett Scott,
Song title

Two roads diverged in a wood, and I—
I took the one less travelled by,
And that has made all the difference.

Robert Frost (1874-1963)
'The Road Not Taken'

Good-bye-ee!-- Good-bye-ee!
Wipe the tear, baby dear, from your eye-ee.
Tho' it's hard to part, I know,

I'll be tickled to death to go.
Don't cry-ee – don't sigh-ee!
There's a silver lining in the sky-ee.
Bonsoir, old thing! Cheerio! Chin-chin!
Nahpoo! Toodle-oo! Good-bye-ee!

R P Weston (1878-1936) & **Bert Lee** (1880-1947) 'Good-bye-ee!'; 1915 song

It's coming – something frightful like a kitchen dragging a village behind it.

Gabriel García Márquez (b.1928)
One Hundred Years of Solitude
(The old woman sees a train for the first time)

The woods are lovely, dark and deep.
But I have promises to keep
And miles to go before I sleep.
And miles to go before I sleep.

Robert Frost (1874-1963)
'Stopping by Woods on a Snowy Evening'

Before he sets out, the traveller must possess fixed interests and facilities to be served by travel.

George Santayana (1863-1952)

There is nothing so educational as travelling

Anita Loos (1893-1981)
Gentlemen Prefer Blondes

The doors had been closed at once, but the train did not move until evening. We had learnt of our destination with relief. Auschwitz: a name without significance for us at that time but at least it implied some place on this earth.

Primo Levi (1918-1987)
If This is a Man

Ah, the delirious weeks of honeymoon!
Soon they returned, and, after strange adventures,
Settled at Balham by the end of June.

Rupert Brooke (1887-1915)
'Sonnet Reversed'

Well, Dorothy and I are really at London. I mean, we got to London on the train yesterday as the boat does not come clear up to London but it stops on the beach and you have to take a train. I mean, everything is so much better in New York, because the boat comes right into New York, and I'm beginning to think that London is not so educational after all.

Anita Loos (1893-1981)
Gentlemen Prefer Blondes

They are lonely
While we sleep, lonelier
For lack of the traveller
Who is now a dream only.

Edward Thomas (1878-1917)
'Roads'

Travel is like adultery: one is always tempted to be unfaithful to one's own country. To have imagination is inevitably to be dissatisfied with where you live. There is in men, as Peter Quennell said, 'a centrifugal tendency.' In our wanderlust, we are lovers looking for consummation.

Anatole Broyard (1910-1990)
'Being There'

We shall not fray or fail. We shall go on to the end. We shall fight in France, we shall fight on the seas and oceans, we shall fight with growing confidence and growing strength in the air, we shall defend our island...

Sir Winston Churchill (1874-1965)
Speech in the House of Commons, 4 June 1940

I told Piggie that when you are travelling, you really ought to take advantadges of what you can not do at home.

Anita Loos (1893-1981)
Gentlemen Prefer Blondes

I reached Turin 19 October after thirty-five days of travel; my house was still standing, all my family was alive, no one was expecting me. I was swollen, bearded and in rags, and had difficulty in making myself recognized.'

Primo Levi (1918-1987)
The Truce

At hawthorn-time in Wiltshire travelling
In search of something chance would never bring,
An old man's face, by life and weather cut
And coloured, - rough, brown, sweet as any nut, -
A land face, sea-blue-eyed, - and hung in my mind
When I had left him many a mile behind.

Edward Thomas (1878-1917)
'Lob'

Certainly, travel is more than the seeing of sights; it is a change that goes on, deep and permanent, in the ideas of living.

Miriam Beard (b.1901)

Never, never, never believe any war will be smooth and easy, or that anyone who embarks on the strange voyage can measure the tides and hurricanes he will encounter.

Sir Winston Churchill (1874-1965)
Accredited

Wherever we go, across the Pacific or Atlantic, we meet, not similarity so much as 'the bizarre'. Things astonish us, when we travel, that surprise nobody else.

Miriam Beard (b.1901)

I travel light; as light,
That is, as a man can travel who will
Still carry his body around because
Of its sentimental value.

Christopher Fry (b. 1907)
The Lady's Not for Burning, Act 1

If you are what you eat, a visit to North Carolina could make you a very interesting person.

North Carolina Travel Department
advert in 1986

God! I will pack, and take a train,
And get me to England once again!
For England's the one land, I know,
Where men with Splendid Hearts may go;
And Cambridgeshire, of all England,
The shire for Men who Understand;
And of that district I prefer
The lovely hamlet Grantchester.

Rupert Brooke (1887-1915)
'The Old Vicarage Grantchester'

Travel is the most private of pleasures. There is no greater bore than the travel bore. We do not in the least want to hear what he has seen in Hong-Kong.

Vita Sackville-West (1892-1962)
Passenger to Teheran, ch. 1

The travel writer seeks the world we have lost—the lost valleys of the imagination.

Alexander Cockburn (b. 1941)
'Bwana Vistas' *Harper's* (New York, August 1985)

Travel can be one of the most rewarding forms of introspection.

Lawrence Durrell (1912-1990)
Bitter Lemons

'The age of independent travel is drawing to an end,' said E.M. Forster back in 1920, when it had been increasingly clear for decades that the mass production inevitable in the late industrial age had generated its own travel-spawn, tourism, which is to travel as plastic is to wood. If travel is mysterious, even miraculous, and often lonely and frightening, tourism is commonsensical, utilitarian, safe, and social, 'that gregarious passion,' the traveller Patrick Leigh Fermor calls it, 'which destroys the object of its love.' Not self-directed but externally enticed, as a tourist you go not where your own curiosity beckons but where the industry decrees you shall go. Tourism soothes, shielding you from the shocks of novelty and menace, confirming your prior view of the world rather than shaking it up. It obliges you not just to behold conventional things but to behold them in the approved conventional way.

Paul Fussell (b. 1924)
'Travel, Tourism, Etc.', *Thank God for the Atom Bomb and Other Essays*

Writing and travel broaden your ass if not your mind and I like to write standing up.

Ernest Hemingway (1899-1961)
Letter, July 9, 1950

Journeys, like artists, are born and not made. A thousand differing circumstances contribute to them, few of them willed or determined by the will—whatever we may think.

Lawrence Durrell (1912-1990)
Bitter Lemons

Exploration belongs to the Renaissance, travel to the bourgeois age, tourism to our proletarian moment...The explorer seeks the undiscovered, the traveller that which has been discovered by the mind working in history, the tourist that which has been discovered by entrepreneurship and prepared for him by the arts of mass publicity...If the explorer moves toward the risks of the formless and the unknown, the tourist moves toward the security of pure cliché. It is between these two poles that the traveller mediates.

Paul Fussell (b. 1924)
'From Exploration to Travel to Tourism'

Travel, which was once either a necessity or an adventure, has become very largely a commodity, and from all sides we are persuaded into thinking that it is a social requirement, too.

Jan Morris (b.1926)
'It's OK to Stay at Home' *NY Times*

It would be nice to travel if you knew where you were going and where you would live at the end or do we ever know, do we ever live where we live, we're always in other places, lost, like sheep.

Janet Frame (b. 1924)
'The Day of the Sheep', *You Are Now Entering the Human Heart*

Years ago, not long after I first arrived in Britain, I remember wandering into a bookshop and being startled to find a section devoted to walking guides. Where I came from we didn't walk much, but at least we could do it without instructions.

Bill Bryson (b. 1951)
The Guardian, March 3, 2001

Travel is not compulsory

Jan Morris (b.1926)
'It's OK to Stay at Home' *NY Times*

In America there are two classes of travel—first class, and with children. Traveling with children corresponds roughly to traveling third-class in Bulgaria. They tell me there is nothing lower in the world than third-class Bulgarian travel.

Robert Benchley (1889-1945)
'Kiddie-Kar Travel', *Pluck and Luck*

'Son,' the old guy says, 'no matter how far you travel, or how smart you get, always remember this: Some day, some where,' he says, 'a guy is going to come to you and show you a nice brand-new deck of cards on which the seal is never broken, and this guy is going to offer to bet you that the jack of spades will jump out of this deck and squirt cider in your ear. But, son,' the old guy says, 'do not bet him, for as sure as you do, you are going to get an earful of cider.'

Damon Runyon (1884-1946)
Guys and Dolls

Sometime, this year or the next, the prospector would arrive at a Brazilian village with news of his discovery. The disasters of the Messinger expedition would not have passed unnoticed. Tony could imagine the headlines that must have appeared in the popular press; even now, probably, there were search parties working over the country he had crossed; any day English voices must sound over the savannah and a dozen friendly adventurers come crashing through the bush.

Evelyn Waugh (1903-1966)
A Handful of Dust, ch. 6

We were madly conserving money for the big day in Dieppe. Esmond noticed a sign at one farmhouse for 'home-made oil'. He inquired from the farmer whether the oil would be suitable for use in the car, which was needing to be re-oiled at every stop. The farmer answered that it would serve excellently as a motor oil, so, since it was extraordinarily cheap, we loaded up with it. After that, the car began going slower and slower. First we were passed by all the other motor traffic; then by cyclists; finally, as we approached Dieppe, little girls rolling their hoops whizzed by us...

We regretfully decided to leave the car parked on a Dieppe street. It really wasn't working any more.

Jessica Mitford (1917-1996)
Hons and Rebels, ch. 19

'What matters it how far we go?' his scaly friend replied.
'There is another shore, you know, upon the other side.
The further off from England the nearer is to France—
Then turn not pale, beloved snail, but come and

join the dance.
Will you, won't you, will you, won't you, will you join the dance?
Will you, won't you, will you, won't you, won't you join the dance?

Lewis Carroll (1832-1898)
The Mock Turtle's Song, *Alice's Adventures in Wonderland*

About fifteen miles below Monterey, on the wild coast, the Torres family had their farm, a few sloping acres above a cliff that dropped to the brown reefs and to the hissing white waters of the ocean. Behind the farm the stone mountains stood up against the sky. The farm buildings huddled like little clinging aphids on the mountain skirts, crouched low to the ground as though the wind might blow them into the sea. The little shack, the rattling, rotten barn were grey-bitten with sea salt, beaten by the damp wind until they had taken on the colour of the granite hills.

John Steinbeck (1902-1968)
'Flight', *The Long Valley*

Burley, who had spent most of the day drowsing in a litter carried by porters, trying to overcome his valley lassitude, awoke one afternoon screaming. He had dreamt that the expedition was starving on Rum Doodle. He produced his calculations and checked them over carefully. It was as he feared. Due no doubt to his attack of London lassitude he had forgotten to allow food for the return journey. Concentrating as he did on the one objective of placing two men on the summit of Rum Doodle, he had forgotten to bring them back again.

I saw that this crisis would tax all my resources as a leader. I said nothing to the others but carried my burden alone for a week, searching for a way out. At last I was forced to disclose the emergency. Wish gave one look at Burley – and I like to think that even in this crisis one of us, at least, was able to spare a thought for the unhappy author – and commenced to scribble on his thumb nail.

'The solution is quite simple,' he announced. 'Dismiss all but 153 porters and 19.125 boys. The food saved will see us through.'

W E Bowman (1912-1985)
The Ascent of Rum Doodle

Set up in Bali, Ko Pha-Ngan, Ko Tao, Borocay, and the hordes are bound to follow. There's no way you can keep it out of Lonely Planet, and once that happens it's countdown to doomsday.

Alex Garland (b.1970)
The Beach

One can never read all the books in the world, nor travel all its roads.

Anonymous

Of all possible subjects, travel is the most difficult for an artist, as it is the easiest for a journalist.

W H Auden (1907-1973),
'The American Scene', *The Dyer's Hand*

Ours is the century of enforced travel…of disappearances. The century of people helplessly seeing others, who were close to them, disappear over the horizon.

John Berger (b. 1926)
'Ev'ry Time We Say Goodbye'

The thought of the return journey stuck in my heart, and I cruelly pictured to myself the inhuman joy of that other journey, with doors open, no one wanting to flee, and the first Italian names…and I looked around and wondered how many, among that poor human dust, would be struck by fate. Among the forty-five people in my wagon only four saw their homes again; and it was by far the most fortunate wagon.

Primo Levi (1918-1987)
If This is a Man

Oh, my. I'd forgotten how much I hate space travel.

C3PO
as the Millennium Falcon takes off, *Star Wars*

Man is an artifact designed for space travel. He is not designed to remain in his present biologic state any more than a tadpole is designed to remain a tadpole.

William S Burroughs (1914-1997)
'Civilian Defense'

Americans are rather like bad Bulgarian wine: they don't travel well.

Bernard Falk (1943-1990)
Quoted in *Observer* (April 27, 1986)

Thanks to the interstate highway system, it is now possible to travel across the country from coast to coast without seeing anything.

Charles Kuralt (1934-1997)
On the Road

...there isn't a train I wouldn't take,
No matter where it's going.

Edna St Vincent Millay (1892-1950)
'Travel'

And yet the road is ours as never theirs:
Is not one gift on us alone bestowed?
For us the joy of joys, O Pioneers!
We shall not travel, but we make the road.

Helen Friedlander
Votes for Women, 1910

Everybody is always planning to go travelling. It is one of those activities, like writing a book, that is filed under for 'one day'. In the 18th century, it was fashionable to do the Grand Tour of Europe. Today, it can be anywhere, and increasing numbers of people are taking the radical step of reinventing themselves as temporary nomads.

Emily Barr (b. 1972)
The Guardian (February 5, 2000)

If you're going to America, bring your own food.

Fran Lebowitz (b. 1951)
'Fran Lebowitz's Travel Hints'

There is a cheap literature that speaks to us of the need of escape. It is true that when we travel we are in search of distance. But distance is not to be found. It melts away. And escape has never led anywhere. The moment a man finds that he must play the races, go to the Arctic, or make war in order to feel himself alive, that man has begun to spin the strands that bind him to other men and to the world. But what wretched strands! A civilization that is really strong fills man to the brim, though he never stir. What are we worth when motionless, is the question.

Antoine de Saint-Exupéry (1900-1944)
Flight to Arras, ch. 12

I sometimes think that Thomas Cook should be numbered among the secular saints. He took travel from the privileged and gave it to the people.

Robert Runcie (1921-2000)
Archbishop of Canterbury

To infinity, and beyond!

Buzz Lightyear
Toy Story

If a man would travel far along the mystic road, he must learn to desire God intensely but in stillness, passively and yet with all his heart and mind and strength.

Aldous Huxley (1894–1963)
Grey Eminence, ch. 9

Soon, we will be fitted with our space suits. Then, it's off to Baikonur. I don't mind admitting that I am looking forward to our lift off with a certain amount of anticipation. Sometimes, it seems that my entire career has been aimed at this moment. The important thing is to use the time remaining as intensely as possible. But we have to make sure that at the end of it we still have the energy we need to do our jobs in orbit. And we will have. I'm confident.

Roberto Vittori, 11 March 2002
Diary of an Astronaut, prior to embarking on a Soyuz 'taxi' flight to the International Space Station, 25 April, 2002

A way of certifying experience, taking photographs is also a way of refusing it—by limiting experience to a search for the photogenic, by converting experience into an image, a souvenir. Travel becomes a strategy for accumulating photographs.

Susan Sontag (b. 1933)
On Photography, ch. 1

One cannot but be surprised by the beauty of the earth

Valentina Tereshkova (b. 1937)
First woman in space

It will free man from the remaining chains, the chains of gravity which still tie him to this planet.

Wernher von Braun (1912-1977)
'On the meaning of space travel', *Time*

Call on God, but row away from the rocks.

Indian proverb

What childishness is it that while there's
breath of life
in our bodies, we are determined to rush
to see the sun the other way around?

Elizabeth Bishop (1911-1979)
'Questions of Travel'

The air traveller is not free. In the future, life's passengers will be even less so: they will travel through their lives fastened to their (corporate) seats.

Jean Baudrillard (b. 1929)
Cool Memories, ch. 3

A journey is like marriage. The certain way to be wrong is to think you control it.

John Steinbeck (1902-1968)
Travels With Charley: In Search of America, part 1

Quite suddenly my two feet were up above my head and I just registered the fact that – golly – this was zero gravity – when the cosmonaut next to me said 'Let go of the bar'. So I opened my fingers and just like that I was up on the ceiling – it was absolutely profound surprise…I absolutely loved this…because you could just give a little kick against the side of the plane and you could fly the length of the plane like Superman.

Professor Susan McKenna-Lawlor
Interview, *Woman's Hour*, BBC Radio 4, 16 June 2003

So every journey that I make
Leads me, as in the story he was led,
To some new ambush, to some fresh mistake:
So every journey I begin foretells
A weariness of daybreak, spread
With carrion kisses, carrion farewells.

Philip Larkin (1922-1986)
'Nursery Tale'

When he was a crawler he left your feet to journey to the sofa and bring you a ball. When he was a toddler he left your side to journey across the grass and bring you a leaf. When he was a pre-school child he left your yard to journey next door and bring you back a neighbor's doll. Now he will journey into school and bring you back a piece of his new world...His journeys are all outwards now, into that waiting world. But he feels the invisible and infinitely elastic threads that still guide him back to you. He returns to the base that is you, seeking rest and re-charging for each new leap into life.

Penelope Leach (b.1937)
Your Baby and Child, ch. 6

Men fall off mountains because
They have no business being there
That's why they go, that's why they die

Sid Marty (b. 1944)
Abbot

I looked down at where I had placed my last ice screw in a boss of water ice protruding from a fractured and melting ice wall 35 feet below me. If I fell now I would drop 80 feet and I knew the ice screw would not hold me. The ice boss would shatter and it would be instantly ripped out. It had quickly become apparent that the route was in poor condition. Lower down I had found myself moving from solid ice onto a strange skim of water ice overlaying soft, sugary snow. It was just strong enough to hold my axe picks and crampon points but it would never hold an ice screw. Hoping for an improvement I had climbed higher and moved diagonally towards the right side of the wall. Then the ice began to resemble something more commonly found furring up the icebox in my fridge. I moved tentatively over rotten honeycombed water ice and onto frightening near-vertical slabs of rime ice – a feathery concoction of hoarfrost and loosely bonded powder snow. It was now impossible to down-climb safely and I tried to quell a rising tide of panic as I had headed gingerly towards the ice boss that was gleaming with a wet blue sheen near where a rock buttress bordered a rising curtain of ice.

Joe Simpson (b. 1960)
The Beckoning Silence, ch. 1

Never criticize a man until you've walked a mile in his moccasins.

American Indian proverb

Not so many years ago there there was no simpler or more intelligible notion than that of going on a journey. Travel—movement through space—provided the universal metaphor for change.... One of the subtle confusions—perhaps one of the secret terrors—of modern life is that we have lost this refuge. No longer do we move through space as we once did.

Daniel J Boorstin (b. 1914)
The Image, ch. 3

In Antarctica... foreground and background were difficult to establish... On shelf and plateau the vision was of an immutable nothingness.

Stephen J Pyne (b.1959?)
The Ice: A Journey to Antarctica

Traveller take heed for journeys undertaken in the dark of the year.
Go in the bright blaze of Autumn's equinox.

Margaret Abigail Walker (b. 1915)
'October Journey'

Senta: These boats, sir, what are they for?

Hamar: They are solar boats for Pharaoh to use after his death. They're the means by which Pharaoh will journey across the skies with the sun, with the god Horus. Each day they will sail from east to west, and each night Pharaoh will return to the east by the river which runs underneath the earth.

William Faulkner (1897-1962)
Land of the Pharaohs

I may not have gone where I intended to go, but I think I have ended up where I intended to be.

Douglas Adams (1952-2001)
The Long Dark Teatime of the Soul

If conquerors be regarded as the engine-drivers of History, then the conquerors of thought are perhaps the pointsmen who, less conspicuous to the traveller's eye, determine the direction of the journey.

Arthur Koestler (1905-1983)
The Sleepwalkers, part 1, ch 2, section 4

How strange a vehicle it is, coming down unchanged from times of old romance, and so characteristically black, the way no other thing is black except a coffin—a vehicle evoking lawless adventures in the plashing stillness of night, and still more strongly evoking death itself, the bier, the dark obsequies, the last silent journey!

Thomas Mann (1875-1955)
Death in Venice, ch. 3

If wishes were horses, beggars would ride

Proverb

Consider a man riding a bicycle. Whoever he is, we can say three things about him. We know he got on the bicycle and started to move. We know that at some point he will stop and get off. Most important of all, we know that if at any point between the beginning and the end of his journey he stops moving and does not get off the bicycle he will fall off it. That is a metaphor for the journey through life of any living thing, and I think of any society of living things.

William Golding (b. 1911)
'Utopias and Antiutopias'

Lost at night in an immense forest, I only have a small light to guide me. A man appears who tells me: 'My friend, blow out your candle in order to find your way.' This man is a theologian.

Alfred Döblin (1878–1957)
Journey to Poland, ch. 10

Keep five yards from a carriage, ten yards from a horse, and a hundred yards from an elephant; but the distance one should keep from a wicked man cannot be measured.

Indian proverb

Oh it's home agin and home again, America's for me!
I want a ship that's westward bound to plough the rolling sea
To the blessed Land of Room Enough beyond the ocean bars
Where the air is full of sunlight and the flag is full of stars.

Henry van Dyke (1852-1933)
'America for Me'

I have recently been told that I am one of the millions of Americans who will be afflicted with Alzheimer's Disease...I now begin the journey that will lead me into the sunset of my life.

Ronald Reagan (b. 1911)
New York Times November 6, 1994

Robert Swan, who walked to both Poles, told me that going to either is like watching a child's magic slate wipe away your life as you knew it.

Sara Wheeler
Terra Incognita, Introduction

Saturday September 19th
Class 4D's trip to the British Museum

7am Boarded coach

7.05 Ate packed lunch, drank low-calorie drink.

7.10 Coach stopped for Barry Kent to be sick

7.20 Coach stopped for Claire Neilson to go to the Ladies.

7.30 Coach left school drive.

7.35 Coach returned to school for Ms Fossington-Gore's handbag.

7.40 Coach driver observed to be behaving oddly.

7.45 Coach stopped for Barry Kent to be sick again.

7.55 Approached motorway.

8am	Coach driver stopped coach and asked everyone to stop giving 'V' signs to lorry drivers.
8.10	Coach driver loses temper, refuses to drive on motorway until 'bloody teachers control kids'.
8.20	Ms Fossington-Gore gets everyone sitting down.
8.25	Drive on to motorway.
8.30	Everyone singing 'Ten Green Bottles'.
8.35	Everyone singing 'Ten Green Snotrags'.
8.45	Coach driver stops singing by shouting very loudly.
9.15	Coach driver pulls in at service station and is observed to drink heavily from hip flask.

Sue Townsend (b.1946)
The Secret Diary of Adrian Mole aged 13 3/4

It was one of those golden mornings of Naples. Within minutes of chugging out of the harbour, the town behind us was afloat in layers of mist, and all its strong colours, its reds and its corals, faded to a pacific grey. After that a headland with pines showing like a pencil drawing, the tops of towers, the Castel Sant' Elmo in suspension over the town, then utter dazzlement. Frazer produced a loaf and cut it up to cries of girlish delight. This party was as much about bread as it was about Capri – an excuse for the ladies to eat limitless white bread under picnic conditions. They munched the bread and laughed uproariously, and threw mangled crusts to the escorting seagulls. An unlicensed fishing-boat veered nervously away trailing a little mandolin music, and ahead Capri penetrated a quilt of mist like the tip of a vulcano.

Norman Lewis (1908-2003)
Naples 44

The boat did it. I was just the pilot...I can't explain how I feel because I don't know myself. But I do know I'm happy to finish today

Ellen MacArthur (b.1976)
Finishing the Vendée Globe, *Guardian*, February 12, 2001

I hold that it is the duty of a man to see other lands but love his own

E V Lucas (1868-1938)

I'm not planning polar expeditions because they've all been done: every single one of them has been done. There are only two poles and me and my rivals from Norway and places have been battering away at them for 30 years and the only ones left are gimmicky: you have to go by camel or motorbike or [something] to be first. So the genuine firsts - supported and unsupported - are all now done.

Sir Ranulph Fiennes (b.1944)
quoted *January Magazine*, October 2001

Mad dogs and Englishmen go out in the midday sun

Noël Coward (1899-1973)
'Mad dogs and Englishmen'

I went for the rig check, which involves climbing the mast, and checking over everything up there before we plunge into the Southern Ocean. It's not easy alone, as the boat never wants to sit still, and there's no one to winch you up, nor ease you down. That's the hardest part of the exercise.

We have a jumar arrangement, like climbers, where as I climb it goes up with me so I'm always attached - then a separate one I ease down with me (not so easy!). On the first attempt I discovered a problem with the genoa stay, which meant I had to go back up - already bruised, I was bit annoyed. When I was up there the wind picked up as I was on my way down. I could have walked down the mainsail if it had been windier.

Ellen MacArthur (b.1976)
diary of Vendée Globe, Day 21,
Observer, Feb 11 2001

I'm astounded by people who want to 'know' the universe when it's hard enough to find your way around Chinatown.

Woody Allen (b.1935)

One of the most adventurous things left to us is to go to bed.

E V Lucas (1868-1938)

A man's feet should be planted in his country, but his eyes should survey the world.

George Santayana (1863-1952)

Exile: one who serves his country by living abroad, but is not an ambassador.

Ambrose Bierce (1842-c.1914)
The Devil's Dictionary

Into the thin and clean reviving air. Over the edge, far down, Wadi Sobale pursued uninhabited windings between gnarled cliffs. But over the plain a silver mistiness made every distance gentle in the sun: our journey lay flat and far and visible before us, flanked, like an avenue, by brown truncated mounds. Flints of palaeolithic man lay strewn here, glistening on the ground; and I thought of the Archaelogist with a gleam of warmth; grateful for the pleasure of now recognising these small and intimate vestiges of time.

Freya Stark (1893-1993)
Winter in Arabia

Absence makes the heart grow fonder

Proverb

A few more whacks of the ice axe, a few very weary steps, and we were on the summit of Everest.

Sir Edmund Hillary (b. 1919)
High Adventure

Well, we knocked the bastard off!

Sir Edmund Hillary (b.1919)
to George Lowe on descending from the summit of Everest, 29 May 1953
Nothing Venture, Nothing Win

The Crowning Glory – Everest is climbed

Newspaper headline, 2 June 1953

Flying may not be all plain sailing, but the fun of it is worth the price.

Amelia Earhart (1897-1937)

Beautiful! Beautiful! Magnificent desolation.

Buzz Aldrin (b.1930)
On seeing the moon

One small step for man, one giant leap for mankind

Neil Armstrong (b.1930)
Takes the first step on the moon

Life ought to be a struggle of desire toward adventures whose nobility will fertilize the soul.

Rebecca West (1892-1983)
Attributed

Beam us up, Mr Scott

Captain Kirk
Star Trek

Travel is only glamorous in retrospect.

Paul Theroux (b.1941)
Observer, 7 October 1979

Commuter – one who spends his life
In riding to and from his wife;
A man who shaves and takes a train,
And then rides back to shave again.

E B White (1899-1985)
The Commuter

Natives dislike speed, as we dislike noise, it is to them, at the best, hard to bear. They are also on friendly terms with time, and the plan of beguiling or killing it does not come into their heads. In fact, the more time you can give them, the happier they are, and if you commission a Kikuyu to hold your horse while you make a visit, you can see by his face that he hopes you will be a long, long time about it. He does not try to pass the time then, but sits down and lives.

Karen Blixen (1885-1962)
Out of Africa

When in Rome, do as the Romans do

Proverb

Whenever I travel I like to keep the seat next to me empty. I found a great way to do it. When someone walks down the aisle and says to you 'Is someone sitting there?' just say, 'no one - except the Lord.'

Carol Leifer (b.1956)

But this journey had beggared our language. No words could express its horror.

Apsley Cherry-Garrard (1886-1959)
The Worst Journey in the World

I got that same feeling as when you look over a cliff and you get that little jolt in your heart - there's lots of that. But in a funny, sick kind of way, it's a good feeling. It tells you you're still alive, your heart's still beating. That's when the best feelings come: when you've dealt with a situation like that and you've come out in good shape. After the worst feelings, you feel great again.

Emma Richards (b. 1975)
Youngest sailor to complete 'Around Alone',
Guardian, October 7 2002

It's the world that's gone mad and had a war while I've just been sitting quietly in my tent

Pen Hadrow (b 1962)
rescued from the North Pole after his record-breaking walk, quote of the week, *Independent on Sunday*, 26 May 2003

It is necessary to travel, it is not necessary to live

William S Burroughs (1914-1997)
Accredited

A perfect storm

The meteorological term for describing the worst possible storm at sea.

The flight from Lake Natron to Naivasha was *Das Ding an sich.* We took a bee-line, and kept at twelve thousand feet all the way, which is so high that there is nothing to look down for. At Lake Natron I had taken off my lambskin-lined cap, now up here the air squeezed my forehead, as cold as iced water; all my hair flew backwards as if my head was being pulled off.

Karen Blixen (1885-1962)
Out of Africa

Travel broadens the mind

Proverb

I can't do very much celebrating here. I do have a few bottles of Bud Light but I'm saving it for the landing. There's no one here to drink it with - that's the nature of solo flights.

Steve Fossett
First solo around the world balloon flight
quoted *Guardian,* 2 July 2002

A rolling stone gathers no moss

Proverb

We arranged our bivouac about 8 feet below that of Heckmare and Vorg. We managed to drive a single piton into a tiny crevice in the rock. It was a thin square-shafted piton. It held after only a centimetre, but it was just jammed. Obviously, once we hung our whole weight on it, it would very likely work loose with the leverage. So we bent it downwards in a hoop, till the ring was touching the rock. In this way, we did away with any question of leverage and knew we could rely on our little grey steely friend. First we hung all our belongings onto it, and after that, ourselves.

There was no room to sit down. The 'Ramp' was very narrow and very steep at this point; but we managed to manufacture a sort of seat with the aid of rope-slings, and hung out some more to prevent our legs dangling over the gulf. Next to me there was a tiny level spot, just big enough for our cooker, so we were able to brew tea, coffee and cocoa. We were all very much in need of liquids.

...It was absolutely no exaggeration to say we all felt quite well and indeed comfortable. Experienced Climbers will understand that statement and laymen must simply believe it...Dry clothes, a reliable piton and precious, revivifying drinks – that is true happiness where the North Face of the Eiger is concerned.

Heinrich Harrer (b.1912)
The White Spider

He travels fastest who travels alone

Proverb

Look before you leap

Proverb

Thursday's Child has far to go

Traditional rhyme

As I was going to St Ives
I met a man with seven wives

Traditional rhyme

I like long walks, especially when they are taken by people who annoy me.

Noël Coward (1899-1973)

Eternal Father, Strong to save,
Whose arm hath bound the restless wave,
Who bid'st the mighty Ocean deep
Its own appointed limits keep;
O hear us when we cry to thee,
for those in peril on the sea.

Hymn

What we're getting is a whole new order of sexual fantasies, involving a different order of experiences, like car crashes, like travelling in jet aircraft, the whole overlay of new technologies, architecture, interior design, communications, transport, merchandising. These things are beginning to reach into our lives and change the interior design of our sexual fantasies. We've got to recognize that what one sees through the window of the TV screen is as important as what one sees through a window on the street.

J G Ballard (b. 1930)
interview (September 1970)

Been there, done that, bought the T-shirt

Proverb

Man your ships and may the Force be with you.

Star Wars

We can't all be Marco Polo or Freya Stark but millions of us are travellers nevertheless. The great travellers, living and dead, are in a class by themselves, unequalled professionals. We are amateurs and though we too have our moments of glory, we also tire, our spirits sag, we have our moments of rancour...But we persevere and do our best to see the world and we get around; we go everywhere.

Martha Gellhorn (1908-1998)
Travels with Myself and Another

After nine days...I'd gotten used to the horizon, to the orderly rhythm of the ship, and all of a sudden the world came flooding back. I found myself looking at Nova Scotia and thinking about my mortgage.

Sarah Ballard
On Bermuda-Nova Scotia sailing competition, *Sports Illustrated,* 1 October 1984

As I walked out one midsummer morning

Laurie Lee (1914-1997)
Book title

I went on to the southernmost town in the world. Ushuaia began with a prefabricated mission house put up in 1869 by the Rev. W. H. Stirling alongside the shacks of the Yaghan Indians. For sixteen years Anglicism, vegetable gardens and the Indians flourished. Then the Argentine Navy came and the Indians died of measles and pneumonia.

The settlement graduated from navy base to convict station. The Inspector of Prisons designed a masterpiece of cut stone and concrete more secure than the jails of Siberia. Its blank grey walls, pierced by the narrowest slits, lie to the east of the town. It is now used as a barracks.

Bruce Chatwin (1940-1989)
In Patagonia

As you are not unaware, I am much travelled. This fact allows me to corroborate the assertion that a voyage is always more or less illusory, that there is nothing new under the sun, that everything is one and the same, etcetera, but also, paradoxically enough, to assert that there is no foundation for despairing of finding surprises and something new: in truth, the world is inexhaustible.

Jorge Luis Borges (1899-1986)
Extraordinary Tales

I come from a very middle-class family of lawyers and architects. Travel was an immense relief – it got rid of the pressure from above and from below. If you are out on the road, people have to take you at face value.

Bruce Chatwin (1940-1989)
to Michael Ignatieff, quoted in *Bruce Chatwin* by Nicholas Shakespeare

Shanghai! Montevideo! Alice Springs! Do you know that places only yield up their secrets, their most profound mysteries, to those who are just passing through?

Salman Rushdie (b.1947)
The Moor's Last Sigh

While armchair travellers dream of going places, travelling armchairs dream of staying put.

Anne Tyler (b.1941)
The Accidental Tourist

Life is a car park

Bob Cripps (b.1951)
Renowned Book sales rep

Our hearts are light and gay because now it's happening, it's starting, we're travelling again.

Martha Gellhorn (1908-1998)
Travels with Myself and Another

The truth is out there

The X-Files

Good-bye. Farewell. Au revoir.

Traditionally said to those taking their leave.

Acknowledgements

I would like to thank everyone who has so generously helped me with this book: particular thanks go to Sarah Such for her kindness, skill and patience. Also to Sarah Gardner, Jenny Calcutt and everyone at Cadogan Guides. I would also like to thank Jon Wood, Katy Follain, Antony Topping, Ali Robertson, Gill Paul, Ophelia Field, Laura Brockbank, Jenny Colgan, Jim Gill, Catherine Trippett and James Crawford.

Source Acknowledgements

The editor and publishers gratefully acknowledge permission to reproduce copyright material in this book:

The Lady's Not For Burning © Christopher Fry reprinted with kind permission of Dramatic Copyrights Ltd

A Room with a View by E M Forster by kind permission of The Provost and Scholars of King's College, Cambridge and the Society of Authors as the literary representatives of the Estate of E M Forster

The Voyage Out by Virginia Woolf by kind permission of The Society of Authors as the Literary Representative of the Estate of Virginia Woolf

The Go-Between by L P Hartley by kind permission of The Society of Authors as the Literary Representative of the Estate of L P Hartley

'Travel, Tourism, Etc.' and 'From Exploration to Travel to Tourism' © Paul Fussell reprinted by kind permission of the author

Winter in Arabia by Freya Stark by kind permission of John Murray (Publishers) Ltd

Hons and Rebels by Jessica Mitford by kind permission of Victor Gollancz

The Beach by Alex Garland reproduced by kind permission of Penguin Books Ltd

Out of Africa © Karen Blixen printed by kind permission of The Rungstedlund Foundation

William Burroughs reprinted by kind permission of The William S. Burroughs Trust

'Abbot' © Sid Marty reprinted by kind permission of the author

The Time Machine by H G Wells by kind permission of A P Watt Ltd on behalf of The Literary Executors of the Estate of H G Wells

The Shadow of the Shark, All Things Considered, The Innocence of Father Brown and The Rolling English Road by G K Chesterton by kind permission of A P Watt Ltd on behalf of The Royal Literary Fund

Little Gidding by T S Eliot by kind permission of Faber & Faber

'Riding Down to Bangor' by George Orwell (Copyright © George Orwell), by permission of Bill Hamilton as the Literary Executor of the Estate of the Late Sonia Brownell Orwell and Secker & Warburg Ltd

The Secret Diary of Adrian Mole Aged 133/4 by Sue Townsend by kind permission of The Random House Group Ltd

The Beckoning Silence by Joe Simpson, published by Jonathan Cape. Reprinted by kind permission of The Random House Group Ltd

Bruce Chatwin by Nicholas Shakespeare, published by Jonathan Cape. Reprinted by kind permission of The Random House Group Ltd

The Ascent of Rum Doodle by W E Bowman, published by Pimlico. Reprinted by kind permission of The Random House Group Ltd

Death in Venice by Thomas Mann, published by Martin Secker & Warburg. Reprinted by kind permission of The Random House Group Ltd

The Moor's Last Sigh by Salman Rushdie, published by Jonathan Cape. Reprinted by kind permission of The Random House Group Ltd

In Patagonia by Bruce Chatwin, published by Jonathan Cape. Reprinted by kind permission of The Random House Group Ltd

'Nursery Tales' by Philip Larkin by kind permission of Faber & Faber

The Young Visiters by Daisy Ashford, published by Chatto & Windus. Reprinted by kind permission of The Random House Group Ltd

Grey Eminence by Aldous Huxley, published by Chatto & Windus. Reprinted by kind permission of The Random House Group Ltd

A Hundred Years of Solitude by Gabriel Garcia Marquez, published by Jonathan Cape. Reprinted by kind permission of The Random House Group Ltd

A Handful Dust by Evelyn Waugh (copyright © Evelyn Waugh 1934) by kind permission of PFD on behalf of the Evelyn Waugh Trust

'Good-bye-ee' by R P Weston and Bert Lee by kind permission of EMI Music Publishing

The Sleepwalkers by Arthur Koestler (copyright © Arthur Koestler 1959) by kind permission of PFD on behalf of the Estate of Arthur Koestler

The Worst Journey in the World by Apsley Cherry-Garrard by kind permission of Macmillan (UK)

'The Road Less Travelled' and 'Stopping by Woods on a Snowy Evening' by Robert Frost from *The Poetry of Robert Frost* edited by Edward Connery Lathem, published by Jonathan Cape reprinted by kind permission of the The Random House Group Ltd Group Ltd and by kind permission of Henry Holt Publishers (US)

'Reveille' from *A Shropshire Lad* by A E Housman by kind permission of the Society of Authors as the literary representative of the estate of A E Housman

'Kiddie-Kar Travel' and 'Carnival Week in Sunny Las Los' by Robert Benchley by kind permission of the estate of Robert Benchley, Nathaniel Robert Benchley, Executor

The White Spider by Heinrich Harrer (copyright © Heinrich Harrer 1959) reprinted by kind permission of HarperCollins Ltd

Black Lamb and Grey Falcon by Rebecca West, first published as a Canongate Classic in 1993 by Canongate Books Ltd, 14 High Street, Edinburgh, EH1 1TE. Copyright (©) Rebecca West 1940, 1941

'The Ship of Death' by D H Lawrence by kind permission of Pollinger Limited and the Estate of Frieda Lawrence Ravagli

A Passenger to Tehran by Vita Sackville-West reproduced with kind permission of Curtis Brown Group Ltd on behalf of the Estate of Vita Sackville-West. Copyright Vita Sackville-West 1926

A Book of Escapes and Hurried Journeys by John Buchan by kind permission of A P Watt on behalf of Lord Tweedsmuir and Jean, Lady Tweedsmuir

'Portraits of Islands' by John Betjeman by permission of The Estate of Sir John Betjeman

Flight to Arras by Antoine de Saint-Exupéry by kind permission of The Random House Group Ltd and Harcourt Inc.

Gentlemen Prefer Blondes by Anita Loos (© 1924) by kind permission of Abner Stein for the Anita Loos Trust

'Mad Dogs and Englishmen' by Noël Coward copyright (c) The Estate of Noël Coward by kind permission of Methuen Publishing Limited

The Importance of Living by Lin Yutang © 1995 by Lin Tai Yi and Hsiang du Lin by kind permission of HarperCollins

Naples 44 by Norman Lewis (c) 1978 by kind permission of Eland Books and by permission of the author c/o Rogers Coleridge & White Ltd, 20 Powis Mews, London W11 1JN

Travels With Charley and 'Flight' from *The Long Valley* by John Steinbeck by kind permission of Curtis Brown for the Estate of John Steinbeck

If This is a Man and *The Truce* by Primo Levi by kind permission of Time Warner Books

Guys and Dolls by Damon Runyan © 1932 by kind permission of Constable & Robinson Ltd

On Photography by Susan Sontag by kind permission of Penguin Books Ltd

Your Baby and Child by Penelope Leach by kind permission of Dorling Kindersley Ltd

Bitter Lemons by Lawrence Durrell by kind permission of Faber & Faber

'Utopias and Anti-Utopias' by William Golding by kind permission of Faber & Faber

Travels with Myself and Another by Martha Gellhorn by kind permission of Penguin Books Ltd

'The Day of the Sheep' from *You Are Now Entering the Human Heart* by Janet Frame by kind permission of Curtis Brown Ltd, London, on behalf of Janet Frame, © Janet Frame

'Travel' by Edna St Vincent Millay. From *Collected Poems*, HarperCollins. Copyright 1921, 1948 by Edna St Vincent Millay. All rights reserved. Reprinted by permission of Elizabeth Barnett, literary executor

'The American Scene' from *The Dyer's Hand* by W H Auden by kind permission of Faber & Faber

Terra Incognita by Sara Wheeler by kind permission of The Random House Group Ltd

'Questions of Travel' by Elizabeth Bishop by kind permission of Farrer, Straus, Giroux

Any errors or omissions in the above list are entirely unintentional. If notified the publisher will be pleased to make any additions or amendments at the earliest opportunity.